Lean Not on Your
UNDERSTANDING

(A mother's journey from loss to recovery)

FRANCES HART

LHA Publishing Co.

ISBN: 0985347902

ISBN 13:   9780985347901

Dedication

This book is dedicated to Gail, my precious daughter who fulfilled all my dreams of what a daughter should be. She enriched my life beyond description and lived the true meaning of her name, "a source of joy." Gail was beautiful, smart, kind, generous, loving, funny, energetic, warmhearted and my cherished friend. She was the link that completed our close-knit family circle. Life without her physical presence is a monumental challenge and unwavering struggle.

Heaven has to be celebrating. Gail will always be loved and cherished. Her presence was our family's joy.

Acknowledgment

The sweet memory of my daughter, Gail demands that I write this book. By helping someone else, I acknowledge that we are still soul mates. Gail was such a giving spirit.

I am grateful to many people who have participated in my earthly journey. Thank you to my mother, Margaree W. Parks, who taught me the true meaning of unconditional love and standing tall regardless of the circumstance. Her talk and her walk were always consistent and true. My mother gave me the courage to write this book by the strength she has always displayed whether the ride was smooth or bumpy. Even when grief engulfed me, I knew I had to try because I was always taught that giving up was not an option.

I am blessed beyond my dreams. I have the support of my husband, Linwood (Lenny) of forty-six years. His love and support keep the wind in my sail. Wherever I choose to sail, I know I will have enough wind for the trip.

I acquired courage from my adult son, Lin, Jr. as he coped with returning, after a ten year hiatus, to college as a fulltime student and football player. He was a study in courage, fortitude and vision. The Saturday before final exams were to begin, his first semester, he lost his only sibling, Gail. Earthly angels surrounded him. One was his football coach who upon hearing of the death of Gail contacted each of his instructors. He arranged for Lin to take his final exams the following semester. Eighteen months later with family and friends applauding, Lin, Jr. walked across the stage, flipped his tassel, and received his degree. He struggled those two years, but with God, strength, character and courage he won the victory.

I am blessed with two granddaughters and a grandson. Their presence in my life, through this book writing process, has taught me the beauty of the renewal of life. I marvel at the innocence and love that is the essence of a child. They have blessed me with unstoppable hope and the love that only a grandparent knows.

God blessed me with the best friends the world has ever seen. I will not name them individually, but they know who they are and whose they are. My friends and the heavenly angels lifted me up when I was so numb, I could not feel my feet under me. They may have gotten tired but they displayed the patience of Job. My gratitude and thanks for my friends and family is unending.

TABLE OF CONTENTS

Part I.

REALITY/THE EYE OF THE STORM

The Eye of the Storm is a place of comfort for those who have lost a child. It is from here that you begin to realize that the feelings and experiences you are having are normal in this moment of great loss. This section also serves to enlighten those who may not have experienced the loss of a child. It is this awareness that will enable them in their efforts to assist others through the storm.

My understanding of this phase came only after numerous encounters with others who faced similar circumstances as a parent, friend, or close relative. When God takes your child, it hits like the violent, whirling winds of a tornado and swiftly leaves you with devastation and heartbreak. . Everything down to the core of your being has been shattered and you are all alone, with the question that has no answer. Where do I go from here? You are completely off balance and out of focus. If only there was someone there, who had walked in the shoes I was wearing at that moment, if only I could have been reassured that what I am experiencing, is normal.

It took time, buckets of tears, continuous prayer, and discussions with people who had been confronted with a similar experience to come to this conclusion. Who needs to also wonder if you're losing yourself? Your plate is piled so high that an army could be fed off it and you would still have leftovers. Unfortunately, you are without an appetite for life.

This section of the book may seem a bit bizarre to those of you who have not lived this nightmare. I thank God you can't relate. However, you will be better able to help someone who has by reading this section . I'm asking you to trust me and the other people who have been there. I find no pleasure in being dramatic, but I do want to make it plain. You think you know, but you don't. I too once thought I was a compassionate, caring person when a friend or relative I knew was forced to start over after losing such a cherished gift as a child. I was as far from the reality of the experience as the east is from the west.

I marvel at the friends and family members who seem to have a sense of the magnitude of the life changing challenge that you must wrestle with daily. The number isn't large, but this is truly one of God's Miracles that anyone would be blessed with that level of insight and compassion. Maybe they're angels.

As you progress through Part I of this book, keep two things in mind: "Reality" comes from the root word real. When you are "In the Eye of the Storm" the rainbow is unimaginable and inner turmoil is your reality. If you're dealing with the loss of your child or want to help someone who has, you have "to keep it real". By that I mean you can't be concerned with other people's expectations or society's definition of where you are or where you should be. You have to deal with you on your terms. Your circumstance is unique to you and you must navigate your own path.

The second thing you must keep in mind was so elegantly stated by Frederick Douglass "If there is no struggle, there is no progress." Every moment has turned into a struggle for you. Tenacity with this struggle will determine your progress. The mere fact that you are willing to struggle is a victory. Bravo for you.

Chapter 1

LOSS OF A DIFFERENT KIND

L oss is something we experience all our lives. We lose baby teeth, youth, innocence, hair, weight, money, looks, friendships, love, jobs, opportunity, freedom and a million other things that are a part of the fabric of everyday life. Loss should be a familiar companion. When it's your child it's like being attacked by a stranger. Your soul screams, but nobody hears. Help is on the way. It won't arrive until all your feelings, beliefs, hopes and cares have been attacked and put on life support as you struggle to survive. You are so numb you can't feel a thing and the scary part is that you can't envision a better day. You go through the rituals of saying goodbye and the public thinks and says you're holding up well. You're in a state of shock and months and years down the road, you'll wonder how you existed that first month or more. You just follow orders. Be here at noon, we'll pick you up at two, service will start at three and on and on. You respond like a programmed robot, but you don't have a clue. Your joy has flipped flopped to tragedy with the blink of an eye.

Exhaustion has suddenly become your constant companion. No matter how you try, your mind is in a never-ending marathon. It continues to race through tears, valleys, despair and hopelessness. Two-three hours of sleep is all you're going to get, so you continue to drag through another day. The routine does not deviate. You pray, toss and turn for hours, finally fall asleep for two-three hours, wake up exhausted and start another day. Hope is something you no longer possess. Your initial reaction upon awaking each morning is disbelief. Like a programmed robot you start another day's journey.

Our family had been overjoyed with anticipation of the arrival of our second granddaughter. My daughter and I talked daily and usually more than once a day even though we lived 250 miles apart.

I always found myself in the baby department whenever I went shopping. It was like I had radar that guided me. I was on automatic pilot or something. I don't know, but I was having the time of my life. I went to stay with my daughter a week before her precious baby arrived and my husband and I stayed a week afterwards. During this stay we celebrated Thanksgiving Day and our 32nd wedding anniversary on the same day. Our new granddaughter took a gigantic leap toward recovery from a lung condition she was born with. The day was so filled with blessings that I could hardly contain my joy and thanksgiving. Occasionally I had a distraction from the overwhelming joy I was consumed with.

One such moment was when Gail and her dad had one of their famous, intense debates, which they both seemed to thrive on. This particular debate was about today's music versus the music of the sixties and seventies. Clearly the generation gap was not going to allow for a meeting of the minds, but both of them would jump in with gusto. To an outsider it would be perceived as an argument. Experience had taught me that they truly loved these no-win debates and they adored each other beyond words. I loved the fact that they could have these exchanges and be none the worse for wear. These debates usually ended the same way. Gail sitting on her dad's lap proclaiming, I love you dad, and her dad beaming from ear to ear replying, I love you too, baby girl.

My husband, Lenny and I returned home several days later because both our granddaughter and her mom were well on their way to full recovery. We continued our daily phone visits. A week later my husband left town for several days on business out-of-state. Around noon Gail called and said she was going to the hospital to see a doctor. I told her to hang up because I was going to see if I could get a flight. It was snowing on both ends and because of the weather I wasn't sure if I could. I got a flight, called her right back and she told me she had to run because her girlfriend, Shelly, was there on her lunch hour to watch the baby and she was in a rush. I told her I'd see you around 6 o'clock. I said, "I love you sweet pea" and she said, "I love you more".

I left my husband, Lenny a message to let him know my plans and caught the last flight out of St. Louis before the airport shut down all outgoing flight because of the snowstorm. I was skating on thin ice because the Kansas City Airport shutdown also shortly after my arrival. When I arrived in Kansas City the weather had turned into a blizzard, but I was so excited about spending time with my daughter and her new baby that nothing else mattered. Gail's friend met me at the airport and as we got near her apartment and the hospital she had gone to earlier in the day, he said let's stop and see Gail. My reply was, oh, they're keeping her overnight. I don't recall whether he answered or not because the road was in terrible shape with the heavy snowfall and the music was blasting.

Immediately I thought of my new granddaughter, Brianna and looked forward to caring for her until we picked up Gail the next morning. My greatest joy in life is caring for an infant and I was ecstatic with the thought of our three generations sharing time together.

I arrived at the hospital, got her room number and walked with a bounce in my step because every moment with Gail was a joy. I could assure her that her baby was in good hands and we'd be back tomorrow morning to take her home. I remember walking through these double doors and being met immediately by a priest and a nurse. You're Gail's mother? I said yes. The nurse said we're doing everything we can for her, but she's fighting for her life. I screamed to the top of my voice, where's my "baby girl" and they said calm down. God help me I cried. A calm came over me and I said take me to my child. They escorted me to her bedside and my beautiful daughter lay there in a coma hooked up to full life support. This was my child that I had just talked to six hours ago, who was hurrying to see a doctor on her girlfriend's lunch hour. Nothing made sense.

During the next three days, I heard many conflicting stories of what happened. The only thing I know for sure is that she drove herself to the hospital, registered, was "treated" and now is lying here in a coma hooked up to more tubes than I've ever seen. My

7

husband, son, Gail's husband and a large group of her friends stayed up around the clock hoping and praying for the recovery of this young, vibrant, fun loving new mom. Gail never came out of the coma and her earthly journey ended. A decade later we are no closer to knowing the truth about whose medical errors deprived my daughter of her life, my granddaughter of her mother and altered the dynamic of our entire family forever.

My daughter's loss still breaks my heart. Intellectually, I know God knows what He is doing and His Plan for my life I must accept if I truly believe, Thy Will Be Done. I must also tell you, I don't understand His Plan and I don't like His Plan. At this moment I'm lost and don't have a clue how to cope with the loss of my precious daughter.

The following week we planned two services for Gail. The first service was in Kansas City where she was living at the time. Emanuel Cleaver, II, who in 1991 became the first African American Mayor of Kansas City, MO gave the eulogy. Following a distinguished eight year career as mayor he was elected to congress. Cleaver was unanimously elected the 20th Chairperson of the Congressional Black Caucus of the 112th Congress. God gave him a short message that was insightful and compassionate. Our family appreciated his thoughtfulness, time and sincerity. We are forever grateful.

A minister friend of Gail's Husband gave us something that we would cling to many days down the road. He related life to the childhood book, The Little Engine That Could. He challenged us at those difficult moments, and he knew there would be many, to be like the little engine and remember, **I think I can, I think I can.** Somehow he knew we were operating on a tank that was less than full. Gail's Dad and her husband gave brief remarks and thanked everyone for their love and support. The minister asked if anyone else wished to say anything. Without hesitation, I found myself standing at the podium. I've always been a behind the scene person and to this day I can't explain how I got up there and where the words came from.

I'm Gail's Mother, Frances Hart. When I was just a little girl, there was this beautiful little girl in our Sunday school named Gail. At the time, I didn't know anyone with that name, but for some reason I fell in love with that name. Frequently I thought that when I grow up, if God blesses me with a little girl, I would name her Gail. One Sunday after church I went home and searched for this name in a book that belonged to my Mother. I looked up the name Gail and it said in old English in the 1800's it was a nickname for Abigail, but in modern times it's a name unto itself and means "a source of joy". Tonight I say to you that Gail would want us to be joyous and not be sad, because she surely was our "source of joy". Many times over the years I would say to her, you really took your name seriously.

I joined church many years ago when I was 13 years old. My grandfather was a Baptist minister and it was the custom in our family that he would give each grandchild a bible when they gave their life to Christ. He had had a bad stroke before I was born and his penmanship was barely legible. He asked my mom to inscribe in my bible "Onward and upward, heaven is your goal." So I say to you that Gail has reached her goal and is in heaven. It took her only 27 years to reach that goal. The rest of us are just a little slow reaching perfection. When you think of Gail and remember her, remember that she was "a source of joy" and she would want us to be joyous.

I took my seat and not only wondered how I got up there, but where the thoughts came from. My heart did the speaking that night and helped me convey to the world what a joy Gail was to our family and all who knew her.

As I look back I don't know how we managed to do the things that were required. I think we were in a state of shock, so none of this seemed real. We isolated the planning and funeral preparation process from our daughter. With the grace of God, family and friends from near and far we survived.

I've shared my very personal experience with you for one reason. When I say I understand your pain, you need to know that

I do. One of the most annoying experiences is when people say I know how you feel. Whenever I talk with someone who has not buried their child and that cliché falls from their lips, inwardly I scream, no you don't.

As I look back and take inventory of my life, I realize that I was being prepared for this devastating moment from the time I was a small child. The groundwork that a Higher Power was laying out for me to cope with a loss of this magnitude went totally over my head. Now as I reflect and my whole life seems to be glaring back at me, I recognize that I was being prepared all my life. I can recall many instances throughout my life when loss paid me a visit.

The first loss, that seemed monumental to me at the time, took place when I was just four years old. This was such a big deal to me at this tender age.

I vividly recall as a preschool child having to accept the role I was given, even though it definitely was not the role I wanted. This was our largest annual production that included every child en-rolled in our preschool program. These annual productions entailed elaborate costumes and pageantry. This year we were having a Tom Thumb Wedding. I never wanted anything more in my short life than to be chosen to play the role of the bride in her gorgeous floor length gown and beautiful flowing headpiece.

The day finally arrived when the school director announced the various roles. I was heartbroken. All hope of being the bride was forever lost, but no one ever knew. I've never shared this with any-one, including my family. For weeks and throughout the rehearsal period, I was devastated. I put on my best face each day, but I dreaded those afternoon rehearsals.

This production lived up to the weeks of work, sewing, sets and rentals. We all had beautiful gowns to wear and Mother had curled my hair to look elegant with Shirley Temple Curls. I'm sure I appeared to be feeling special the evening of our big performance. No one knew that I was dealing with my first overwhelming loss. I may have been a beautiful little bridesmaid, but that is not the role I wanted or would have chosen. Fifty plus years have passed and My Mother still has a large professional photo of the entire cast that evening. The photo reinforces the fact that I was not the bride and attendance by what seemed liked everyone I ever knew assured that there were many witnesses.

Looking back over my life at this moment of loss, I realize that I've been on this journey for a long time and God has been preparing me to handle loss with strength and dignity for my entire life. I know for sure since I was four years old. At four I walked down the aisle, took my place and smiled with style, grace, strength and dignity. I'm praying constantly, as I'm forced again to accept a role I did not chose and I do not want, for the courage to give a duplicate performance with style, grace, strength and dignity. It gives me a glimpse of hope.

As I reflect on that event so many years ago, I believe that at four God had given me what I needed to cope in my little world and He will give me what I need today. I believe that there's a reason why after putting the Tom Thumb Wedding in my memory bank so long ago that God bought it front and center in my mind today. I hear Him saying, "I've been preparing you all your life for this moment when I would reclaim My Child. You found a way with your limited life's experiences as a four year old and with fifty years to enhance your toolbox you're prepared to make it."

At this stage the preparation seems woefully inadequate. This is one of those occasions when all you can do is "lean not on your understanding". Understanding isn't among your possessions at the moment.

Presently, the overwhelming numbness consumes my total being. I scream why, why, why. Please let me awaken from this nightmare. The first two years I'd awake after a couple of hours sleep. My initial thought would always be disbelief. After talking to other "tornado" survivors, I learned that was the normal response. Our children bury us; we don't bury our children. The natural order of life has been broken, and it's impossible to fix.

As I try to take control of my life, I'm reminded of the Time Square Ball in New York City on New Year's Eve. This ritual marks the passing of the old and the birth of the new. The previous year was wonderful until the ball drops. Suddenly, the old year has less significance. The glory of the New Year offers hope and renewal. These are the ultimate goals I'm seeking.

For as far back as I can remember I always wanted to attain two goals in life: one goal was to become a mother and the other goal was to become a grandma. When I was growing up and people asked me what I wanted to be, I always said a teacher or a nurse. I thought people would think I was over the edge as a ten year old if I admitted my true dream. Thankfully I'm at a place in my life now that I'm not concerned with other peoples' evaluation of me or my dreams. The dream of being a nurse disappeared before I became a teenager because I only wanted to work with children and the thought of losing a child overwhelmed me.

My great gift in life is the ability to love and especially children. The innocence of a child is so refreshing and invigorating. They also teach us that the little things and tasks are important. Have you observed a toddler helping to bake cookies or learning to set the table? It's important, intense work and a pure joy to witness.

We must grasp that ability, once again, to find joy in the little forward steps we make as we try to refresh and invigorate ourselves. This too is serious, intense work. The effort seems gigantic and the results seem oh so small. You must step out on faith, as you continue on the path to your new undefined life. As painful as it is to admit, the old life is gone and embracing this new one is the granddaddy of all challenges, but it's all we have.

Regina Belle's Song "A Whole New World" that was sung at Gail's Wedding will forever have new meaning. Her childhood friend sang that song as she and her new husband strolled out of the church after exchanging their vows, I envisioned the birth of a new wonderful life for our precious daughter and prayed that all her dreams would be fulfilled. I can say with certainty that one of her dreams that she had since she was a preteen did come true: having a daughter. She dreamed of this precious child for most of her life. Nobody ever loved a child more than she loved her beautiful daughter. What a short earthly journey they shared. Today I don't have a mental picture of what this new world is for me, but I know I would have never chosen it for myself. Life chose it for me and life isn't something that is dictated by humans. The Almighty makes that call.

....

"To climb steep hills requires slow pace at first".

WILLIAM SHAKESPEARE

....

Chapter 2

BROKEN ORDER

"So since I'm still here livin', I guess I will live on. I could've died for love, but for livin' I guess I was born."
LANGSTON HUGHES

B*roken order* is a term that is probably not found in the dictionary, and when I use it, I'm not talking about the natural order of loss that we usually take for granted. We acknowledge and accept as we reach the age of maturity that we will one day lose our grandparents, parents, and eventually our own lives, as we too will depart from this earth one day. Even this concept or reality is something that takes years to embrace. Young children believe that Mommy and Daddy will always be around to care for and protect them from the hurt and the pain of this world. As a young child, I felt completely safe and secure when Daddy was at home. It's wonderful that we don't have to see the world through adult eyes initially. Thank heaven for that brief period of time when we experience the world through the innocent mindset of a child.

Broken order here refers to the loss of a child. All the maturity in the world seems inadequate when summoned at that tragic moment in time. The impact and the daily struggle are overwhelming when you lose a child. "Mentally all-consuming" is the only way to describe your present state. Long-term coping is out of the question. The shock of the experience is like comparing an April shower to a hurricane. Unless you've been there, you don't know. You may think you know, because you're a compassionate person, or you have lost a loved one also. I can say with fervor, your best estimation is that it's a thunderstorm. Hurricane never crossed your mind. That's okay. Every time someone says to me that they can't imagine what the loss of a child is like, I say, "Thank God." Misery does not love company in this situation. Thank God you can't imagine. Broken order isn't something that you're asking, wanting, or hoping for anyone to understand. You're hoping they don't, because that means that individual has never buried a child. Thank heavens.

However, the last thing you want to hear is someone telling you they know how you feel and then going on to tell of the loss of a grandparent, parent, or other relative who had already outlived the normal lifespan. These are two different animals. The loss of a child is not the same as the loss of an elder—just as an elephant is not a dog, even though they're both animals.

After several years of struggling, I now know that this is one of the few events in the course of life that you must conquer without any real preparation. This conclusion was verified by complete strangers and relatives who had endured this experience. My now-elderly aunt buried four of her children when I was a child and young adult. Her family suffered, but they maintained dignity. That overwhelms me. One day I was at the mall close to where I live at a jewelry store, and I had Gail's six-month-old daughter with me in her stroller. The lady said, "Your daughter is beautiful." I said, "This is my granddaughter." She said, "Are you babysitting for the day?" The strangest aura seemed to be in the store. It was if time stood still. We talked for twenty minutes, and no one came into the store. She shared with me that ten years prior, she was in a horrible car accident and was in a coma for six weeks. When she finally awoke, she learned that her two-year-old daughter had died and already been buried. When her daughter was born, she was told she couldn't have any more children. I never saw that lady again, but she taught me that even without preparation, you can and must go on. I met another lady at that same mall, who shared her story of losing twin boys three years earlier, also in a car accident. I vaguely remembered the story from the news. It seemed as though God was pulling strangers together for comfort and sharing. Sharing is something you aren't likely to do unless you have been there. I could go on and on, but I'm sure you get my point.

The game of life is tricky. You're forced to play this game with dignity and courage, and you don't even know the rules. Where do I start, and how do I proceed? We live in a society where we plan even simple events. We make a reservation for something as simple as a meal, or we buy tickets in advance for a sporting event or a musical performance. With the loss of a child, you have to figure out the rules of the game and play simultaneously. Without the benefit of the rules, you don't have a clue when you're playing well or when you're losing ground. No one comes to you and says your game is bad. Each day you enter the stadium of life and try to engage in the game. All sense of order has escaped your life—but boy, are you trying. You have never given so much for so little. Each day you seem to be at the same place, but you continue trying to press forward. For a very long time, you are taking baby steps.

The first rule I learned and fully appreciated about this part of the game was that taking baby steps is okay. At least you are not losing ground. This was a huge breakthrough for me. Now I'm playing in a game with at least one rule. It's a start. This one rule is monumental when you're in the shock of the loss of your most precious gift, and inner turmoil is your new reality. This inner turmoil is constant and has arrived on your doorstep with more than one piece of luggage. That's your first clue that your stay in this place will not be short.

The initial stage of wrestling with this all-consuming loss can't be given a time frame. I wish there was a neat little timeline to pass on to you, but each situation has a separate course to run. Each relationship has a history that has never existed before and can never be duplicated. That's why loss can never be compared. So why are comparisons offered up so freely?

It took me a year and a half before I got through a complete day without crying. I was doing the absolute best that I could, and I could not take on the responsibility of worrying about whether I was making progress or not. I was praying for help, guidance, peace, and hope as I devoted every ounce of strength that I had to moving forward. I accepted that I was doing what my parents had always stressed: "Give your best." Frequently your best will seem inadequate, but keep trying anyway.

During this period I was reminded of a statement a minister use to make when I was a little girl. At the time it had little meaning, but now I realize that it was put in my memory bank for a reason. He simply said, "Keep on keeping on." This is profound advice. One day you will surprise yourself and discover that you are moving forward, be it ever so slowly. Pause, give thanks, and give yourself a big hug.

At this stage you will even experience erratic moments of the gift of peace. My dear friend Shirley gave me wonderful, insightful advice that has served me well over the last few years. She told me, about twelve months after Gail completed her earthly journey, that peace is something that you can't sustain, so enjoy it for the moment. That was good advice. Peaceful moments and days come and go. Peace approaches like a shooting star and makes its exit just as suddenly. Savor the moment.

Remember that school, church, company, or reunion picnic that you attended and, two sides were chosen to play tug-of-war? The long rope with the huge knot on both ends is the key to the game. The teams line up, and the game begins. Suddenly your life feels like you're the rope. You're pulled back and forth, back and forth between the past you loved and the unknown future that awaits you.

Memories are the only certainties in your life. You have precious memories that, in time, will make your heart sing again and bring a smile to your face, but that day is many tears away. Robert Louis Stevenson, the Scottish writer, defines our challenge thus: "Life is not a matter of holding good cards, but of playing a poor hand well."

Memories at this stage remind you that they're all you have, and moving forward is taxing, because your future dreams are missing a key player. Life waits for no one, and the cards have been dealt. You must gather your cards and play the best you can today.

Tomorrow will be a new day, and the level of your play will vary from day to day—much like the weather in Missouri. One day the sun is shining, and the next day you're shoveling snow. Your victory is already claimed by your courage to participate. Life is moving on all around you, because the show must and will go on. It would be so easy to fold your tent and vacate camp. Over time, you will know you are doing the right thing by trying. Today all you know is that you played your hand, and you don't know or care what the results are. You're going through the motions of being involved. As overwhelming as life is at this stage, the reality is that life is for the living. It will take time, but eventually you will actually participate in life again and not just absorb oxygen.

Understand that you have become the tortoise in the race with the hare. You will cross the finish line, but you must allow yourself time, determination, and patience. You have many hopes, dreams, plans, and thoughts to rearrange and develop. The order of life has to be redefined and somehow embraced. Giving this "broken order" some type of shape or form is a tall task. You don't get in shape overnight; likewise, this battle won't be conquered until you have invested more sweat equity than you knew you possessed.

"Broken order" is a mental battle that can quickly become a physical one. The brain and the school principal have many similarities. One similarity is that they both preside—one presides over the human body and the other over the student body. In both cases, it all begins at the top. Mental stress can wreak havoc physically on the body. You must gather every tool available to you and decide that, somehow, you will conquer this unnatural situation you find yourself in. As you approach this quest, understand that it will take prayers, tears, work, time, and maturity. You're not looking for perfection, but hope, resilience, and movement toward a new meaningful life with a purpose.

Three years after God took my daughter to be with Him, I realized that my answer for coping with "broken order" was there, plain as day, in the Lord's Prayer: *Thy will be done.* You must take the focus off of yourself and place it where it belongs. It has always been about God's will, not yours. I frequently say that I'm trying to live in God's will for my life. I don't always understand it, and I don't always like it, but I always have assurance that He knows what His will for my life is. Knowing that His will not my will is the key. This is not an easy task, but if I try to live in my will, I will never be happy again. My will is and always will be to have my daughter here with me. Happiness is my goal.

....

"Perfection is attained by slow degrees;
she required the hand of time."

Voltaire
....

Chapter 3

HAVE YOU EVER?

*"Although the world is full of suffering,
it is also full of the overcoming of it."*

H ELEN K ELLER

One day I was sitting on the edge of the examination table in my doctor's office with my feet dangling, waiting to hear the doctor remove my chart from the door and enter. I was overwhelmed by symptoms. The doctor is about to be bombarded, but he has no idea. After the routine cordial greetings and temperature, pulse, and heart check, he sits on the little round stool in the corner and asks, "How are you feeling today? How can I help you?"

Following a long pause—or as my mom would say, I was trying to "collect myself" and fight back tears—I said, "I don't know where to start." My doctor said, "Take your time, I'm listening." I blurted out, "I lost my daughter two weeks ago, and I know I need to see a doctor, but *have you ever felt hopeless?*" I felt totally devoid of hope for mental peace or physical comfort, and I was holding on spiritually by the thinnest thread that was wrapped around a gigantic *why*. I struggled to explain the unrelenting tightness in my chest that seemed to have found a comfortable home, the tightness in my shoulders that seemed to have an invisible clasp attached to it, the endless nights without sleep, the disbelief that this was real, and my lack of ability to continue in this state. My shoulders, neck, and back seemed so weighted down that it was unbearable.

My doctor was very attentive and compassionate. He allowed me to ramble without interrupting or addressing each complaint. When I finally came to a halt, he expressed sorrow for my loss and explained that my physical problems were probably all stress-related. I had had a complete physical two months prior and was given a clean bill of health. He knew that I didn't suddenly have a complete physical breakdown, even though I was a wreck.

He prescribed a mild sedative, and I took my exhausted self home. I took one of the prescribed pills and felt like I was floating. I didn't like that feeling, either, so I decided that I was not going to become dependent on prescription drugs. My doctor would not have let me do that, anyway.

In retrospect, I realize that I wasn't completely out of control, because I was able to have a rational thought concerning prescription drug dependency. I definitely couldn't handle another issue. This situation is one where you just have to "go with the flow." I don't mean to suggest for one minute that the flow is smooth, and many times it's not a pretty sight.

A higher power helped me to stay afloat. Many times I felt mentally exhausted, but I was getting through the moment. It took months for the moments to become hours and eventually days. Physically I should have been fatigued, because I could not sleep more than two hours many nights. The comfort of daylight seemed to replenish my energy source. I cannot explain why. My life is full of events that I cannot explain or comprehend. All I can do is accept God's will.

Thy will be done. Embracing God's will gives new meaning to that line in the Lord's Prayer that you've recited a million times. When you're forced to put reality and meaning to words, it's like tasting something special for the very first time. I remember the first time I tasted a Chunky candy bar at about age twelve. I had seen the commercials on television, but when I took a bite of one, it was an entirely different experience. I don't mean to minimize the experience of yielding to God's will, but for some unknown reason, I suddenly remember that bar of candy. I also understand the African Proverb, "Seeing is different from being told." Some things we have to experience to understand and give birth to a new level of life.

There were many occasions when I experienced growth in rebuilding my new life. Frequently it was overshadowed by a song Gail loved, a fragrance she had introduced me to, a look on her daughter's face that so reminded me of Gail, the ring of the phone that, for a split second, I thought was her calling, a glance at her sweet picture with that unforgettable smile, and a thousand little reminders of the wonderful gift that had been taken away. We were soul mates; our lives, thoughts, hopes, and dreams were intertwined. Life without my daughter seemed impossible. Time has taught me that my mother's old saying, "Life is for the living," is true. Regardless of how challenging, the saying is true.

Everything seems to be more profound, and everything takes on new meaning. I hear songs differently that I've listened to a thousand times. In our little church of about 150 members, which I joined twenty-four years ago when I moved to the Midwest from the east coast, the choir used to sing, "Nobody Told Me That the Road Would Be Easy," and I agree. For years it was just a song I enjoyed; now it's a song I live. It embraced me—I didn't embrace it.

"The great thing in this world is not so much where we stand, as in the direction we are going."
OLIVER WENDELL HOLMES, SR.

Chapter 4

HOLIDAY MASQUERADE

"We wear the mask that grins and lies."
PAUL LAURENCE DUNBAR

There are few things that I know with certainty in this life. I know for certain that during the first year following the loss of your child, every holiday will be accompanied by a raging inner storm. Everyone I've talked to—and my own experience—tells me that there is no way around this. You are longing for lost family traditions. You are trying to do something you don't know how to do, and you have absolutely zero interest in celebrating anything. You go through the motions, but you have as much holiday spirit as a robot. The chilling reality is that you're going through the motions while your soul yearns for things to be the way they have been in the past. Silently you scream, *I don't want to celebrate a tradition that has ended.* Our traditional holiday celebration included my daughter.

Gail loved holidays, especially Christmas, with all the decorations, gift giving, and baking that went with it. The only way we got through that first Christmas after burying our precious daughter on December 20th was to concentrate on the fact that it was the birthday of Jesus Christ. We did not want Gail to look down from heaven and see that her one-month-old daughter didn't have a Christmas tree on her very first Christmas. We dug out the tree ornaments and artificial tree around midnight on Christmas Eve and proceeded to decorate it the same as we had the previous year.

Christmas morning we sat our little granddaughter under the tree and prayed. We were truly thankful for the wonderful, darling gift that our daughter had given our family. We had an angel on the top of our tree, but nothing could compare to our little angel sitting at the bottom of our tree. Gail always gave the most wonderful gifts. That one thing had not changed. Warmth and beauty surrounded our precious granddaughter that difficult Christmas Day.

We had many gifts under our tree that our relatives had sent from out of state. We had no family in the Midwest except our son and two granddaughters at that time. Phone calls came in all morning from family members on the east coast. We thanked them for the gifts, but we couldn't be specific, because none of the gifts had been opened. No material item would make any difference. My mother called from Virginia around two in the afternoon, and, being a mom, she sensed that we hadn't opened any gifts. She told us to open our gifts when we finished talking. Like robots, we did as we had been told. I lack the words to describe my feelings that first holiday. Maybe it's because I had none.

The week between Christmas and New Year's Day presented a gigantic test of our ability to cope. I have learned that even the darkest night is followed by daybreak. Through Gail's precious daughter, God revealed His presence with warmth and the hope of a new beginning. Caring for her represented the essence of all that this earthly journey offers. She reminded us that we are all helpless babies, and our total existence is dependent on the loving care of our Father. Lord knows we loved and adored this tiny child. We cared for her with a heavenly love. She represented the new dawn of each day.

The world seemed like it was standing still, but the New Year made it clear that life goes on, regardless of your circumstances.

That first year, it seemed like every time I blinked, there was another holiday staring at me, and they were all the same. Holidays in our family had always been so much fun and filled with sharing and surprise. Suddenly, holidays turned into dreaded days. I didn't know how to celebrate without my daughter, and I didn't care. I was just numb. Suddenly many of them seemed like a gigantic commercial joke. Valentine's Day is a perfect example. I don't need to be told when to express love to my family and friends. As that first year progressed, holidays just kept rolling on.

Easter took me on a merry-go-round of memories. Not only did I revisit the birth, life, death, and resurrection of Jesus, but I was consumed with the cycle of my daughter's life. I was still in the "why" stage of her being taken and expecting an answer.

A friend I've known for twenty-five years had tragically lost a son before I knew her. She called me periodically, because she understood the reality of the loss of a child. Her advice to me was that the public gives you about three months to grieve, and after that you just have to go inward. I tried to do as she had suggested.

All my life I've heard people say during difficult periods, "Just lean on Jesus." I continued to go to church. Some Sundays I cried, some I had to leave early, and some of those Sundays I was there physically, but I struggled to focus on the service. One thing I knew was that if it was Sunday, I would go to church.

Mother's Day and Father's Day were like conjoined twins. I don't know which one of these days presented the most gigantic challenge. Daily I was consumed with my loss and trying to be there for Lenny, the love of my life. Each of these days brought hurt and a new experience for my son as well. How could we comfort him, when we were trying to find our center again ourselves? What a balancing act. We have never been circus performers, but we survived. If you ask me how or what was our secret, I don't know.

A month following Father's Day was our daughter's birthday. In our family birthdays were celebrated like formal holidays. We tried to remain positive and commemorate Gail's life. That day we gave our all, but "the mask that grins and lies" ended up on the floor. Bravo, we tried. That first year, the birthdays for the remaining family members were so far from our traditional celebrations that the days just seemed to be another day, and everyone was okay with it.

What a difference a year makes. The year before, Thanksgiving was filled with happiness and blessings. Our granddaughter, Gail's baby, had just turned the corner, heading to a full recovery from a respiratory problem she was born with, my husband and I celebrated our thirty-second wedding anniversary, and life could not have been better.

We went through the motions. I cooked the traditional dinner. Our small family and a friend gathered in our dining room, and we went around the table, as we always did, saying what each of us was thankful for this past year. All was well, except that the elephant in the room was gigantic. We managed to get through the day, elephant and all. The one thing that we were all grateful for was the victory of completing that first year of holidays.

"In my distress I called upon the Lord, and cried to my God; and He did hear my voice out of his temple, and my cry did enter into his ears."

2 S A M U E L 2 2 : 7 , K J V

Part II.

THE CHALLENGE

I learned many lessons along the way. One of the most impactful lessons was learning how to survive during this phase. You must reinvent the wheel. I know you don't feel up to it, but your survival is at stake. You loved the life you had, but it's gone, and you only have two options: try or die. Given that choice, trying is the way to go. I'm not suggesting that this is a clear-cut decision, because trying entails a long, sustained effort and struggle. There will be times when death seems so appealing. There is nothing scary about dying to a Christian. Being with God has been your long-term goal and would be so comforting at this moment, but the timing of attaining that victory is in God's hands, not yours.

Hopefully, those moments when you just want to give up are few, but asking them not to creep in is a bit much at this stage. Thankfully, most of the time, you have the will to press on. I've been there. I will tell you that I chose to try. Giving up or quitting was not an option that my parents had ever taught me. Their lives hadn't always been easy, but they embraced struggle as a part of this earthly journey and never took the defeatist approach. I dared not, either. Even at that lowest point in my life, I had no desire to dishonor their memory by quitting. This life's journey is about so much more than any one individual. We are attached at the hip to all humanity. I admit, some days I don't know how I'm going to carry on, but I know I must; I will, and I hope you will also.

You may have to find that quiet, private place where something from your earlier days will resurface to serve as a model or standard for pressing on with dignity. I'm reminded of how my parents carried themselves when my brother lost his long battle with throat cancer. My dad stood tall, even though he was recovering from a mild stroke, when his mom was hit by a drunk driver and killed instantly. I can't say what happened in their private rooms. but what I saw was them playing the hand they had been dealt with dignity and strength. I will be forever grateful that God blessed me with parents who also served as role models. I was not scurrying around looking for an athlete or celebrity to fill that role. I had dinner each night with my role models. Life does not get any richer than that.

Luckily, I didn't have to struggle with the loss of my daughter alone. I stepped out with faith as my companion. I didn't have to lean on my own understanding for the purpose of my very existence. I discovered that life would shock me without warning. Sometimes the ride is so challenging that I feel like if I hit another bump or curve in the road, I'm out of here. I'm reminded of Langston Hughes's words: "Don't you sit down on the steps, 'cause you finds it's kinder hard."

Nothing about my walk resembled the way I strolled down the hall in high school with a confident attitude. I can't believe that these are the same feet that use to step so high with the college marching band. Patience is golden as I reach into the depths of my soul to discover my next step.

Chapter 5

AM I WHO I SAY I AM?

"I have learned that success is to be measured not so much by the position that one has reached in life as by the obstacles which he has overcome while trying to succeed."

BOOKER T. WASHINGTON

One of the intriguing mysteries of this earthly journey is trying to pinpoint our individual earthly mission. *Why was I sent here in the first place?* It isn't something that I spent a lot of time on in my youth, because that's a time when life isn't meant to be well-defined. As my journey continues, I complete my education and move into the workforce.

No longer are all life's major decisions and responsibilities being managed by my parents, guardians, or some other loving, caring person. Guess what? Life's major decisions and responsibilities are now on my desk, and I am the new manager. I'm sure we all remember playing hide-and-seek as a child, and the action went into high gear when you heard the words, "Ready or not, I'm coming." That's what life is saying to me at this moment. I can't escape the moment; I can either embrace it with the determination of a champion, or it will wrestle me to the ground. Most of us have that champion spirit.

My twenties, many times, find me feeling like I know how to do this adult thing. I have the world in the palm of my hand, I have the answers to just about everything, I'm earning more money than I thought I ever would, and I'm having a good time. My thirties are about to change everything.

My experiences have led me to certain conclusions. Thirty-year-olds are responsible and are planning for the future. Many are even talking about second careers, retirement, and managing retirement plans. Conversations are so much more serious than I remember from a year or two ago. I'm taken much more seriously now, and the beliefs and values that were instilled in me as a child begin to resurface and become constant companions. All the beliefs and values that seemed so stupid and outdated, keeping my parents permanently stuck in a time capsule, are beginning to seem so logical. Amazingly, these are the values and beliefs that I'm suddenly clinging to for dear life. *What's happening to me?* Out of the blue, I may find myself in church, not only on Sunday but also during the week. The center of the universe has shifted, and it's about so much more than just me. I'm trying to understand the Higher Being, as I gradually discover that this journey is complex and frequently a mystery. Where did the carefree twenties go? I don't have the answer to that question, but I do know that they won't come again. Thirty is now on center stage.

I'm embracing a belief system that I honor and daily strive to uphold. This system determines every thought, deed, and action, and I don't compromise it for anything. Going against my belief system is like abusing my very soul. I know who I am, and hopefully it's someone I truly adore and feel comfortable with. This doesn't mean that I'm selfish or self-centered. It means that I love myself enough to be loveable and accept love. Without self-love I have very little to give to others and the world. In the absence of self-love, talent is underdeveloped or wasted, and growth and fulfillment is stunted. This self-defining process is a necessity for developing a strong foundation that I can build and rely on in both the sunshine and the storm. It defines who I am.

Several years ago I was in that place; I had been there for many years. I knew who I was, I loved who I was, and my belief system was firmly in place. I believe in a Supreme Being, heaven, salvation, and a plan that is laid out by a Higher Power. For me that is the One I call God. The name varies from person to person, and that's okay. I am willing to accept His plan for me, because God is the center of my life; and I accept that He certainly knows what's best for me, even when I don't understand it. My mom says that's why it's called *faith*. We trust someone greater than ourselves, who is much more than we can totally comprehend.

I believe the day will come for each of us when we will find out if "I am who I say I am." The question will demand an answer, and the question will be directed to *you*. You must answer it to continue to live a productive, meaningful life. Your response to the question will define the quality of your future and the impact you'll have on this universe. We're all interconnected and need each other. We all desire to be surrounded by positive energy from our fellowman.

My defining moment came fourteen years ago, when I abruptly lost my beloved, only daughter. Gail was my best female friend in this vast universe. I share this personal experience, as well as every word in this book, because I believe it will help somebody to know this: you are not alone.

I never remember a time in my life when I was not in the church. I have been on this faith journey a long time, and you know what? It doesn't matter. This *test* will rock the very foundation of everything you ever thought you knew and believed. It's like going to take that big exam you've been preparing to take for months—in some instances, for years. You walk into the exam room, and your entire mind goes blank. You will be freaked out. Your entire future is before you in a flash, and you don't have a clue as to what your next step should be. Answers to all your questions have escaped you. "I don't know" is your only available response. The questions are numerous, but there are no answers at the moment. Time will render some answers, but many of the answers won't be revealed until we reach that heavenly place. Even that's a revelation.

Gail was so much more than a daughter to me. I absolutely adored her. We were truly soul mates. She had just given our family a beautiful little girl two weeks earlier. We were so thankful and excited about the future and the fact that both of them were doing okay. I spent two weeks with Gail, one week before she gave birth and a week following our granddaughter's birth.

I was now at the moment that no parent ever expects to experience. As soon as I walked through the hospital's double doors to go to her room I was greeted by the nurse and the priest. My heart rate increased. I had no idea what was coming. When I heard she was fighting for her life, I screamed, "God, help me." A fearful and anxious feeling came over me. I was escorted to her bedside, where she was in a coma on full life support machines. I had just talked to her several hours ago before she drove herself to the hospital.

What had they done to my child? The following moments, hours, and days represent a parent's worst nightmare. Parents are supposed to make everything all right and fix things for their children. The helplessness that followed gripped my body, heart, and soul with the force of a lightning bolt. I prayed, begged, and asked God for a miracle. My darling daughter never woke up. Three days later she was gone. I know heaven was brighter than ever, but life for me was darker than midnight in a cave.

At that time I didn't know who I was or what I believed. Logic didn't fit; looking back, I was in such shock and disbelief that I was operating almost in a trance. I think I appeared to be functioning in an acceptable manner. I don't know, and I don't care. I was doing the absolute best I could. Your best is always acceptable. Today's best isn't necessarily tomorrow's best. This is the day of reckoning. The question was staring me in the face, and the letters looked ten feet tall. *Who am I?*

This wasn't one of those easy questions. My entire existence rested on my response. The answer was buried in the depth of my soul. I was fighting for sanity, just to make it through the next hour. Those hours seemed like days, and days seemed like weeks. I was constantly trying to find the motivation to care about moving forward. My only Escape from this living hell came when I finally turned off all the lights and curled up in the middle of the bed with the thickest comforter I could find.

I was attempting to shut out the entire world. At this stage, victories were small. *I had made it through the night, but the morning* had now taken on a new meaning. Daylight arrived and I stopped looking at the lighted dial on the clock radio on my nightstand. I was finally able to bring the tossing and turning to a halt. Physical and mental exhaustion were my two new companions. Looking back, I realized that each day, I had to answer the question, "Am I who I say I am?" The fact that I was still experiencing evenings and daybreaks with a degree of sanity says that I was still in the game.

Answering this question is a long, difficult, gut-wrenching labor of love you must endure to give birth to a new, unidentified life that you really don't want. The familiar comfort zone of your old life has become simply a precious memory. This labor is going to be long, hard, and challenging. It takes an elephant two years from conception to birth, but this may seem very short compared to the time it will take you to emerge into your new world. This process does not have any clear-cut guidelines. If you have a short journey and can build a new, happy, healthy, productive life quickly, then you are the exception.

My point is simple. You must take as long as you need. Time isn't the issue—wholeness is. It has been fourteen years since my beloved daughter left to be with God, and I have covered many painful miles on my journey. I now cope with the loss better most of the time. Sometimes a detour or roadblock will send me racing down a side street of denial, despair, tears, and sorrow that I haven't traveled for a while. Oh, how shocked I am to find myself on these side streets, because I have tried so hard to avoid going there again. The most insignificant occurrence can surprise you and send you down that cold, lonely road.

I recall one Sunday evening when my husband and I had just left a very crowded movie. As we were leaving through the double doors of the theater, my husband said he would be right back and headed toward the men's room. I was standing off to the side, waiting on him so we could go home. Another lady was also waiting for her husband. Her teenage daughter came over and threw her arms around her mom's neck and gave her a hug, exactly the way my daughter used to hug me. Shortly afterward, my husband returned to find me in tears. I regrouped quicker than I would have two years ago, but for a minute, there I was on the street of tears, looking for a way back to the main street. I'm thankful the detour didn't take me too far off the street I wanted to travel.

Eventually you'll find your way back to the main street. There will always be a scar in your heart to remind you of the journey that you are forced to make. A scar from surgery I had when I was two years old reminds me that you can succeed without being flawless. Don't let a blemish from the battle frighten you.

I have wonderful news to share with you. I have discovered that I am truly who I say I am. After mourning, struggling with my loss, evaluating my entire life, and wrestling with this new unknown life, my faith and core values are alive and well. They have sustained me through it all and continue to guide me through each peak and valley. I am forever grateful for my faith in God and the values that my family shared and instilled in me. They are gifts that I treasure. I also know that I will rely on them the remainder of this journey, just as I have done in the past.

Please understand and be very careful not to rush or attempt to arrive at this place on someone else's watch. I've talked to other people who moved along much faster. I also know one lady who after many years is still cursing God for taking her child. I'm thankful that's something I can't relate to. I never cursed God. Each person, in this situation, can only march to the sound of the music he or she hears. You might be out of step with the world's expectations of you. You're on beat to your song, and that's the only song you can sing. Don't be concerned if man judges your progress, because only God's judgment matters. Humans are not qualified and need not apply for that job. In your own time, you too will arrive at the place where you have a positive answer to the question: *Am I who I say I am?*

"*Perfection is attained by slow degrees; it requires time.*"

VOLTAIRE

2 Year old Gail

1st Grade Photo

Gail posing for her first photo shoot (9 yrs. Old)

Gail & her dad Lenny share time together on the girls softball team.

12 year old photo shoot

Family Portrait

A proud and happy moment. Graduation

Here, I'm receiving my Master's degree with my mother,
Margaree W. Parks and Gail

Gail with an adoring glance at her newborn baby girl, Brianna Stanfield

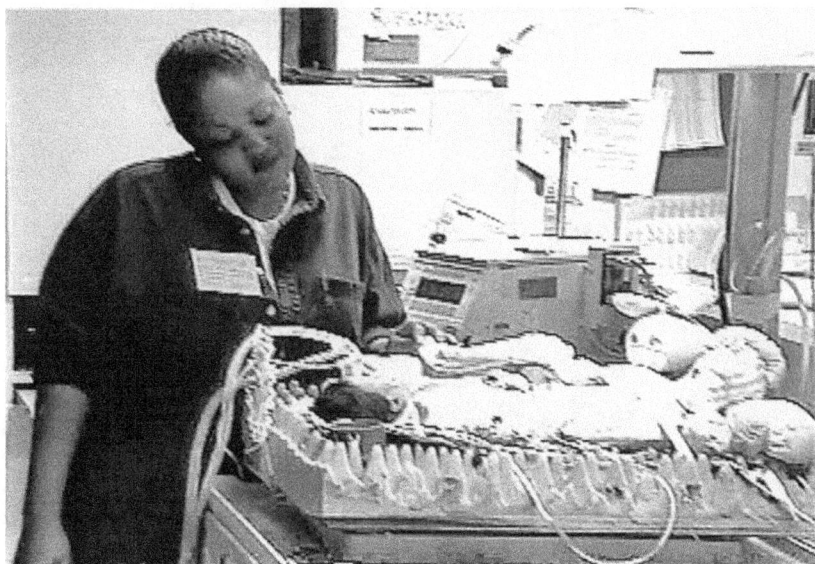

Gail and 3 days old Brianna. (November 28, 1997)

Chapter 6

VISUALIZE A BETTER DAY

"You conquer fate by thought."
HENRY DAVID THOREAU

My husband and I have been happily married for forty-six wonderful years. Over the course of our marriage, we tend to revisit moments that made a profound impression on our lives. My husband, over the years, has revisited the uncanny phenomenon that he experienced in high school and college with regard to his football game performances. He always says that many of his best catches or biggest plays felt like replays. He'd say, "I've seen or done this exact catch or play before." What had happened was that he had visualized making a catch or a certain play, and his subconscious had grabbed that image and stored it. On game day, my husband unknowingly reached back into his subconscious and played out that image. Much of the creativity that we never tap into is permanently stored, waiting to be called on. Watch a group of toddlers or preschool children play. Their creativity seems to be endless, as they play and create for hours. My granddaughter can create an entire meal with water and whatever is available on any given day in her play kitchen. Lack of ingredients is never a factor. Our creativity isn't lost with age, but it isn't called upon as frequently as we mature.

At this point in your life, as you try to survive, you'll have to be tenacious. Take a few minutes and give yourself a mental vacation. Imagine yourself in a calm, relaxed state. Maybe you're relaxing in a warm bath, enjoying a sunny day at the park, lost in your favorite book, or on the beach. You choose the destination. The possibilities are endless.

This may sound like foolishness to some of you. This is a real challenge, because your mind is racing, like a hamster on a wheel. Your continuous mental motion is getting you nowhere. Stopping it long enough to take a mental vacation or getaway is very important. If possible, you can extend this little mental escape beyond a few minutes and gradually increase your getaway time. This will not happen immediately. Time will become your friend. Both your mental and physical health will benefit from these little getaways. This relief from stress will be welcomed with open arms by your body's immune system and your emotional health. In the months and years ahead, when your hope and creativity slowly return, this mini mental vacation will still be available. This is not a limited-time offer with an expiration date. When you need a getaway, book your reservations.

Initially this mental vacation may look totally out of reach or sound ridiculous. Unfortunately I was not only convinced of this— I'm on record not only for thinking, but also for writing that I have no hope for a better day.

In an effort to thank people who reached out to our family in an extraordinary way when we lost Gail, I bought copies of a little inspirational book that I was reading on the airplane while going to Kansas City on the tragic day I learned my daughter was in a coma. In the front of the books, with tears falling down my cheeks, I wrote, "Thank you for your kindness." I also wrote, "I have no hope for a better day." It was impossible for me to visualize a moment when hope would embrace my soul and become a part of my life again. I have no idea why I shared this with my friends, because in hindsight, that seems exceedingly out of character for me. Where did that private person go who was taught as a little girl that what goes on at home stays at home? This surely didn't leave space for sharing my gut feelings. Visualizing life surrounded with excitement, creativity, goals, and enthusiasm was as outrageous as the thought of me landing on the moon.

Time has taught me that answers take time, and survival gives birth to patience. Childhood experiences from my mental warehouse constantly engulfed me. It reminds me of those subjects that we complained about along the way in school. We knew beyond a shadow of a doubt that we would never see or use this "boring stuff" again in life. Twenty years later, at the kitchen table, with your disinterested teenager who is convinced all parents are dumb, you're glad you took algebra. Suddenly this "boring stuff" has real value. If nothing else, it shows your well-informed teenager that you have some intellectual value. Over time, at a snail's pace, little revelations will start to fall into place and make sense.

If possible, I hope you will be able to visualize a better day—and even if not now, I hope a mental snapshot is stored and has become a part of your subconscious. Nothing would make me happier than to recall the freshness of a bright, sunny day with hope streaming across the sky like a message from the Goodyear Blimp. If you're in a hopeless place right now, I'm asking you to reach back into your memory bank to a wonderful day you experienced, before misery stopped by your house. Visualize laughing and tasting the fullness of life.

During this period, my whole life seemed to be on rewind, and then it was as though someone suddenly pushed "stop," followed by "play." It seemed like my subconscious was going through a massive spring-cleaning. Incidents that didn't seem to be that significant or to have been earth shattering years ago began flashing through my mind on a daily basis. Evidently, nothing is ever deleted in the subconscious. It is always there. I have visited my life from preschool to the present. Nothing could shock me anymore. Shock and surprise seem to go with the territory these days. Why all of the childhood flashbacks? I think they're there to remind me of how I have handled difficulties in the past. I am stronger than I ever realized.

I have gone from being in the major league of life back to the little league of life. In a blink of an eye, the playing field has changed. The familiarity of the field is suddenly distorted. My tomorrows, hopes, dreams, and plans have been destroyed and tossed out. My laughter has turned into despair, and my voice isn't recognizable.

My uniform no longer fits. Suddenly I'm small, oh-so-scared, and consumed with a feeling of helplessness. Even walking up to the plate is a challenge. Everything is unfamiliar territory. I'm in a crowd, but I feel all alone. I have become that frightened little person in a new uniform up to bat for the first time. I must participate, because I'm on the team of life. I don't recall signing up—and I'd rather be anyplace other than here at this moment—but this is where I find myself. My swing is weak, but at least I'm swinging.

This is a small part of what I bring to the plate. Gail and I both enjoyed softball as young girls and as teenagers. My coping skills are stronger than I realize. Over the past fourteen years, as I have given it my all to live without my precious Gail, my swing has slowly gotten a little stronger. Occasionally I get a single or walk, and who knows if the future holds a home run for me? Right now singles look and feel good, and I think I might be ready for a double in the not-too-distant future. Some days I am just thankful that God has given me a walk. It sure beats a strikeout.

I recalled that my parents instilled in me that quitting was not an option. Somehow I must take this loss and develop a completely new life. I have never visualized life going on with this kind of pain and emptiness. I have to start over, but I don't know where to start.

Life seems to have a pattern, which took years for me to discover. I do not know if the pattern runs through everyone's life, but it does run through mine. When I am at my lowest point, and it seems like I am at a dead end, a pathway emerges and opens up. I see this small beam of light in the distance that says, "Your life is not totally void of meaning. You have your faith, family, health, intellect, and opportunities that you have not even dreamed of. Most of all, you have the gift of love that you have treasured throughout your life."

I remember being afraid as a little girl to go upstairs alone at night because of the darkness. My brother, who was a few years older than me, would occasionally—when I least expected it—say he'd go upstairs with me. It was usually for something very important, like to get my favorite doll. I can't tell you what relief that gave my little soul and how special that made my brother to me. I would bounce up the steps and back with renewed energy, because I did not have to go alone.

Each time I try to climb out of my despair, God says, "I will go with you." I know He is with me always. Sometimes the mind gets so frenzied with earthly images that it is impossible to visualize and focus on God's presence. He understands and cannot stand to look at me in such a pathetic state. I do know that when I have reached that "rock bottom" place of despair, He reveals His presence to me in a way that gets my attention. These incidents are not always packaged in a way that I would have chosen.

I recall one night when my husband was out of town on business, and I went to Wednesday night Bible Study alone. I have always enjoyed those upbeat classes and left feeling like I learned something new, or like the class had given me a deeper understanding of an old concept. This particular night, out of the blue, I was consumed with grief and longing for my daughter, even though it had been three years since she left for heaven. No matter how hard I tried, I could not focus on the lesson. It got to the point where I just wanted to get up and dash for the door, but I knew that would draw more attention to me than I could stand. I prayed, "Lord, please helps me get through this class and out the door without breaking down in uncontrollable tears." I had numerous friends at this class, but right then all I could think about was getting from my chair to the door. What a gigantic task.

I heard "Amen" from the closing prayer, so it was time to spring into action. I passed one friend, who said, "How are you tonight?" I managed to say I was okay. I was on the move now. As a second friend approached me, I felt like I was losing control. She said, "Are you all right?" The floodgates opened, and tears flowed like the day I laid Gail to rest. The well-thought-out plan of escape was a distant memory, and a small crowd now surrounded me. Eventually I pulled myself together enough to say, "I don't know what to do." My friends didn't have any idea what had taken place in my life. I'm sure my daughter didn't enter their thoughts, because if you haven't lost a child, you don't realize that it takes years to feel like you have both feet on the ground. People see that public mask that you put on as you leave your home and assume you are coping well. I'm thankful they can't see that the wound is still raw and the healing has scarcely begun. Somebody said, "What happened?" I blurted out, "No matter what I do, I can't get over losing Gail." Advice started flowing on things to try, and each time, I blurted out between sobs, "I've tried that." Several offered to drive me home, but I refused. All I could think was, *Why didn't you keep your out-of-control butt home tonight?* About midnight that evening, the little inner voice said, *Don't beat up on yourself. At that moment you were doing the best you could. Your best is sufficient.* The next day I called a number of friends and apologized. I didn't want them to be concerned about me.

The following Sunday I wrestled with whether I could show up at church without being totally embarrassed by the previous Wednesday night. I had vowed to just lean on Jesus from the very beginning. This definitely doesn't mean that I liked or understood anything about God's plan and why He took Gail. I had gone to church every Sunday, starting two weeks after her loss. It didn't matter whether I cried or mentally went astray. I just kept going, Sunday after Sunday, because that was all I knew. I was searching for answers that can't be found down here, but I had to discover this and many other revelations over time. I got dressed for church, reached for my keys, put on my public face, and stepped out in faith.

Experience has revealed to me that my game will improve with time. When the strikeouts get me down, and doubt consumes me, God picks me up, dusts my uniform off, and shows me that He is still walking hand in hand with me. It continues to be a daily challenge, but knowing that I am not alone makes all the difference in the world.

One of the great gifts my mother gave to me was a love of reading. We use to sit around the kitchen or dining room table, reading poetry and prose after we finished our homework. It seems as though I was always reading books and could not put one down once I began. These were truly wonderful moments in our house, and I thought it was the standard in all homes. My husband finds is very humorous when I reminisce about the wonderful times we shared around the table, exploring literature. The humor to him is that we thought this was enjoyable. He says we must have been geeks, but we really were not. My love of reading has taken me through numerous books over these last few years. All mental distractions are welcome.

I ran across a statement by Abraham Lincoln during one of my reading escapes. I knew from history that he had experienced loss on a larger scale than I could imagine, including the loss of children. I have a healthy respect for people who speak from experience and little for those who have all the answers about waters they have never waded in. If your feet are still dry, how do you know the temperature of the water? Lincoln was wet up to his neck. Life had crowned him the undisputed champ of loss. His words engulfed me as I visualized a tomorrow impregnated by hope.

....

"In this sad world of ours, sorrow comes to all, and it often comes with bitter agony. Perfect relief is not possible, except with time. You cannot now believe that you will ever feel better. But this is not true. You are sure to be happy again. Knowing this, truly believing it, will make you less miserable now. I have had enough experience to make this statement."

ABRAHAM LINCOLN
....

Chapter 7

YOU ARE NOT ALONE

....

*"My presence will go with you,
and I will give you rest."*

Exodus 33:14

....

Each of you, while attending a funeral or memorial service, regardless of religious affiliation or lack of one, has heard these familiar words regarding the deceased person's family: *They certainly are holding up well.* Through this most challenging period in my life, I discovered that the Higher Being, which for me is God, put a shield of protection around me so that I could get through the initial period with some dignity and grace. I call it the "protective bubble," and I envision this gigantic padded dome that will prevent breaks, bruises, and scars when we fall and stumble along those first few months. After this period, one day you will wake up and the "protective bubble" has disappeared and been replaced with numbness and shock. It's as though your loss just happened.

This inescapable fall will hit you like the unexpected rumbling of a tornado. You have searched the deepest valleys of your soul for answers, help, relief, belief, faith, hope, guidance, and direction, and the only response is still denial. You go through the motions of living because you have discovered that in general society's window of recovery is woefully short. One day I woke up and found that the total numbness that had become my constant companion had subsided, and reality slapped me to the ground. It was like skating on a frozen pond the way you have done for months, not seeing any change in the temperature, but suddenly you fall through the ice and you're fighting for your life. The chill seems life threatening, and you can't even imagine that you'll ever feel warmth again. You struggle to escape that arctic cold as grief consumes both your body and soul. I've come to believe that God surrounds us in a "protective bubble" until we get through the initial societal stages of dealing with our loss. But the reality must be faced, and the chill of winter has to be endured, before the hope of spring and new life can even be imagined, much less embraced. It seemed as if spring would never come, but there were occasions when I would get a fleeting glimpse of it. This feeling was overshadowed by reminders of the wonderful gift that had been taken away, but at least I still had my friends and family.

One of the things I have tried to do in the last several years is to share my experience with others when I think it will alleviate even the slightest degree of pain. Warning that the "protective bubble" will surely burst is one of those instances. I've learned that this experience goes with the territory. I had the unpleasant occasion of sharing with (or warning) a young couple, on the loss of their young daughter after a devastating illness, that the "protective bubble" would burst in several months. This warning only serves to let you know it's coming, and that you are not going over the edge. It is part of the grieving process that seems to be a well-kept secret. I have discovered, in talking to the thirty-plus people whose lives have intertwined with my life, that this is one of the few consistencies we all experienced in our loss of a child. I have not discovered why it seems to be not spoken of, because the "protective bubble" will burst, and your wounded heart will feel pain like it has never experienced before.

This is important, because during this time, you are always on the edge; and you could easily topple over if you thought this experience was unique to you. This is foreign territory you're traveling. Every step of the way, you are trying to still discover the rules to this game you've been forced to participate in. I don't care how religious or grounded you think you are; the churning and inner turmoil you're trying to cope with will make you feel alone at times. You are so numb, frequently, that you cannot even feel the presence of God Almighty.

It's like being on a treadmill and trying to stand still. You're moving constantly and wondering why God is being so silent. Eventually you'll get so tired that you will jump off the treadmill and stand still. When you stop, you can focus. God wants your undivided attention. Some of you are in better shape physically and mentally than others, so the timing for each individual varies and can't be predicted. Just as friendships come in many forms and serve many different needs, so does our relationship with God. God will reveal Himself in His time, according to the relationship that you have with Him. He revealed His presence to me several times in ways that completely shocked me; His timing was impeccable.

The first occasion happened four months after I lost my beloved Gail. I was desperate to feel God's presence. The night before Easter, I prayed all night long. "Most gracious and all-wise Heavenly Father, I need to know that Gail is with you and in a better place. I need to know that my baby girl is okay. Please answer my prayer and reveal yourself to me." I rambled on and on and on all night. I gave thanks for everything under the sun, prayed for sleep, guidance, patience, hope, and peace. I was so glad when morning came. Totally exhausted and sleep-deprived, I got up at daybreak. I went into the living room to open the drapes. What I saw made me run down stairs to the family room and back upstairs to the bathroom. By this time I was in total shock on one hand and jubilant on the other. In each of those rooms, there were one or two large plants that we had received in honor of our daughter. All the blooms had died shortly after we received them. I have never had a green thumb, and even though the foliage was healthy and thriving, I was convinced they would never bloom again under my care. Most days I was grateful that I had caring friends who had sent them, but other days I resented them, because they symbolized Gail's departure.

Early that Easter morning, as I scurried from room to room, I discovered that each of these large plants had one large white bloom that wasn't there when I went to bed the night before. Momentarily I couldn't believe what I was seeing. This seemed like one of those stories that you might remember hearing when a relative died, and you overheard the old folks talking, when death was still a complete mystery to you. Maybe those stories you overheard were true, and there was no need to be afraid and sleep with the covers over your head for the next month. Right now, all I know is that God answered my prayer by giving me a sign. He revealed His presence and allowed me briefly to experience that "peace that passes all understanding" that the deacons used to refer to all the time in the little church I grew up in.

I woke my husband up and insisted that he come with me throughout the house. I didn't tell him what this little tour was all about, and I knew that he was just indulging his out-of-control wife for the moment. Just as he hadn't missed the blooms when they disappeared several months before, he didn't notice their reappearance in the early morning hour that Easter morning. Of course I shared the entire revelation with him. I've shared this miracle many times.

Several weeks later, in a women's Bible study group, I shared the experience with my friends. As I described the large plants, which I didn't know the name of, one of the ladies told me that these plants are called peace lilies. For a fleeting moment that Easter morning, I experienced the sweet, gentle touch of peace and the assurance that my precious daughter was safely in His arms. It was a miracle I could not anticipate, because my body and soul had been so numbed by grief.

Four months later, on my daughter's birthday, I got up very early. I spent time alone, anticipating getting through the day and longing to hear Gail's voice. I could almost hear her saying, "Hi, what you doing?" on the phone. The telephone was one of our best friends. I put the coffee pot on and sat at the table, praying. Suddenly, from the baby monitor, I heard Gail's precious little eight-month-old daughter moving around. She was like the rainbow in the storm, and caring for her was a total joy. I rushed from the kitchen, because I never wanted her to have to cry for anything. I opened the door to her nursery. There she was, standing with the biggest grin on her face, and then she said, "Hi." This was the first time I had ever heard my granddaughter say a word. I know God heard the longing to hear Gail's "Hi." That was the best "hi" I will ever receive, and I know who sent it. All I could say was, "Thank you, Jesus, and bless your little messenger."

October 8, 2000, my birthday, I was in mental turmoil, missing my daughter and remembering how special birthday celebrations were with her. My granddaughter was now living with her dad, and I didn't think he would remember that it was my birthday. The phone rang, and the sweetest little voice said, "Happy birthday, Maw Maw." It reminded me that God can make earth and heaven smile simultaneously.

I realized that God taking Gail because her mission was complete was not him punishing me. His plan may bring grief, heartbreak, and life-changing challenges to all of us who love her. We don't know, like, or understand His plan. We're human and not God. We also don't know what the end will be, but God does. I think He let me struggle with the *why* of my daughter's loss until I comprehended what living in God's will really meant. We always want to attach punishment to tragedy, or say that God did this or that to get our attention. Bottom line: we don't understand His plan and won't until that day when we stand face to face with Him. The fact that someone reaches the ultimate goal that all Christians claim to be striving for (living in paradise with God) doesn't mean something negative for his or her loved ones. I can guarantee that each of you have had someone say to you that God was either punishing you or getting your attention. I experienced those remarks on several occasions, when I was so fragile and on the edge that I just wanted to scream. Everything isn't about you. It could simply mean someone reached the ultimate goal.

My thoughts traveled back to when I was a teenager. The Platters had a hit song called "The Magic Touch" that everyone loved. As I thought about that song, which had escaped my thoughts for what seems like a lifetime, I thought about my daughter. Everyone Gail touched, she left better than the way she found him or her. She was gifted with the magic touch, and the fruits of her labor have continued to enrich and uplift people she never met—and some who weren't even born yet. Her work was exquisite and complete.

Some people spend time trying to search for blame and punishment in everything, especially loss. I have learned that in some situations, it's simple. The person's mission is complete. Now before I mislead you, you need to know that it took me four years of agony, grief, pain, prayer, observing, analyzing, and searching to grasp the fact that Gail's mission was complete. This reality does not change the agonizing emotional roller coaster that you find yourself on, frequently and without warning. You still miss your child daily, and you would give up everything you have or could ever have to hold your precious gem once more.

God isn't going to reveal the reasons why about your life to an outsider. If He has given you an answer, go with it. If He hasn't, just live in His will and know that on that day, it will all be made clear.

Before daylight Thanksgiving morning, November 22, 2001, I had a dream that was so vivid that I was disappointed when I awoke. I was talking with Gail like so many times before. She said, "Mom, don't worry about Thanksgiving without me physically being present, because I'm home in the presence of Jesus." My reality of Gail's new residence had not changed, but the idea of her being in the presence of Jesus is reassuring. Frequently I would feel like God was not hearing my request for help and understanding. As I look back, I realize that He never let me linger too long. He knew how much I could stand.

· ·

"He let me bend, but he always
rescued me before I broke."

HENRY WADSWORTH LONGFELLOW

· ·

Chapter 8

TURNING WORDS INTO FEELINGS

"And above all things have fervent love for one another, for love will cover a multitude of sins."

1 PETER 4:8, NKJV

My mother taught me countless life lessons by example. One of those lessons didn't seem significant growing up, but if I never use it again, it has served me well as I create my new life. "Consider the source" was uttered without batting an eye whenever words were uttered that would have been better left unsaid. Mothers seem to have a "truism factory," where they manufacture wisdom. This phrase is worth remembering. You have more important battles to fight than the one with words better left unsaid.

Survival is top priority at this point in your life. Instead of walking away being irritated, you'll walk away without wasting mental energy. Lord knows at this stage, you have no energy to waste. Energy is at a premium, and every ounce you can preserve will truly be needed.

This is a time in your life when you must somehow work magic to change awkward, cold words into warm, loving feelings. Frequently, well-meaning friends will test your ability to see through their words to their heart. It takes time to develop this skill. Initially you will find yourself unequipped to interpret many remarks, and your feelings will be crushed. I found myself in tears and hurt more often than I care to remember. That first year I was so close to the edge that a feather could knock me over. This is part of this new life that you don't want, didn't ask for, and you aren't good at yet. *Vulnerable* has become your middle name.

I discovered that after about three months—six months, if you're lucky—people assume your life is back to business as usual. What a joke. You are putting on your best game face as you walk out the door, praying that you can maintain your public mask until you return home. The public has given you that brief period of recovery, so you have to reach inward for survival.

The day before Thanksgiving, after almost a year without Gail, I went to the supermarket. My nerves were on edge, because this would be the first Thanksgiving without her. The previous Thanksgiving was the last holiday we spent with our beloved child. I had been trying to concentrate on my many blessings to get through the holiday. As I approached the checkout line, I looked over two aisles and saw a former neighbor I hadn't seen in three or four years. She waved and shouted across the aisles, "I heard about Gail. I guess you're over that now." Tears flooded from everywhere. God had placed a gentle, kind, compassionate lady as the checker at my aisle. That stranger with her tender spirit helped me regain enough composure to finish checking out and make it safely home. The task of changing those words into warm, loving feelings was way beyond my expertise. I relied on old faithful: "consider the source." This battle with well-meaning words requires more than one weapon for battle.

One lady who had lost her son in a horrible accident over twenty years ago shared a story with me that gave the phrase "insult to injury" new meaning. At her son's service, a longtime family friend approached her and said she knew exactly how she felt. The lady went on to say that the previous month, her cat Felix, who was eighteen years old, had died. She said her family was devastated because Felix was so much a part of the family. Out of the blue, I replied that many people just can't relate, and that's a good thing. She said, "I never thought about it that way, but that would help explain the remark."

From the very beginning, I went to church, because all I knew was to lean on Jesus, and I am blessed to have wonderful, supportive friends there. I was not going to give up, because my Mom had always taught us that life is for the living. "If you woke up this morning, then you're supposed to live." Not that you should try to live, but you are *supposed* to live. It sounded like a requirement, so I continued to try. As I look back over my life, my mother has never told me anything that was wrong or that wasn't in my best interest.

I'm not going to doubt her words now. In fact, I'm leaning on her example and wisdom just to get through the day.

I remember seeing a friend one Sunday morning, following the service. This is a person I have called "friend" for over twenty years. We hugged, and I said, "I haven't been close enough to speak to you for a while." My friend answered, "I've been avoiding you, because you're so gloom-and-doom since your daughter went to be with God. I don't want you to pull me down." This was one of those times that I was equipped for his words. I knew this person would never intentionally hurt me, and this occurred the week after I heard the sermon titled *Living in His Will*. I was able to turn those awkward words into warm feelings over time. I had just accepted that I was living in His will the previous week. Even though I cried all the way home, my recovery was swift. I refused to let anyone rob me of that pristine peace that had eluded me for so long.

The above examples are a little harsher than most. I shared those because there are times when, try as you will, you can't explain what would motivate someone to say certain things. There are times when you are not required to say anything, because there are no words that fit. A hug is good, or a warm smile is appropriate. After a while, most comments will roll off your back so swiftly that the mental energy expended is minuscule. The problem with the frequently used and unsolicited clichés is that they do nothing to address your present situation. If you have something that can assist me through today, then I'm all ears.

Other well-intended friends may offer the following clichés. My experience is that they will provide little comfort, so don't expect any:

- It was her time
- Our days are numbered
- She's in a better place
- At least you have your granddaughter
- She was never yours anyway

- You'll see her again
- She's still with you
- Be thankful for the time you had with her
- Time will heal all wounds
- You must move on

While comforting for some, such sayings offered little comfort in my moment of distress. At this stage of coping, it would be fantastic if we could gift wrap comfort and present it. There is a small gift that I know is invaluable, and I offer it to you: "Love conquers all."

I have been blessed with wonderful friends who were priceless during these challenging years. I realized that, regardless of what others said, they were a gift from God. I was able to turn their words into wonderful feelings. The saying "you hear what you want to hear" is true.

. . . .

"Friends are quiet angels who lift us to our feet when
our wings have trouble remembering how to fly."

ANONYMOUS

. . . .

Chapter 9

EMBRACING "THE PLAN" WITH JOY

*"My brethren, count it all joy when you
fall into various trials."*

JAMES 1:2

One of the many things you will discover is that the answers and revelations have always been present. Frequently we are "out to lunch." As you search your soul for answers, you soon discover that they will not come unless you can learn to be still and listen. Have you ever been in a roomful of people, and everyone thinks the whole world wants to hear their story or opinion? I have. Occasionally at those times I tune everyone out, because it's more about ego and self-importance. I choose not to participate. That doesn't mean I leave the room physically, but the result is the same.

You will discover that God is the same way. He doesn't ever leave us, but He doesn't reach us in the mist of confusion. Over the past several years, God has always been there, even when I didn't recognize Him at the moment. One incident frequently enters my thoughts these days, and I'm extremely grateful. My beloved daughter dropped out of college after her first year. It seemed liked the entire sky was falling, and I couldn't imagine where her head was. She had told us her senior year in high school that she didn't want to go away to college, because she wasn't ready to leave home. There are numerous colleges and universities in the St. Louis area where we live. My husband and I thought going to college locally wasn't an option. We thought going away to college is where you grow, develop independence, and mature into a responsible adult. How could she know what was best? We had wonderful memories of living on campus away from home. We surely didn't want her to miss that experience. Time has a way of altering our memories. I had forgotten that my first two years of college were a mixture of very happy moments and moments of wishing I was any place but there. With the passage of many years, I had chosen to only cherish the good memories and discard the bad ones. Virginia State University, my beloved campus, is where I met my husband.

I also needed to accept the realization that my dreams were not her dreams. How could they be? We grew up in different generations and circumstances, with different opportunities, and the list could go on and on. It seems like a "no-brainer" now. I had been so busy laying out my dreams and expectations for her that I had failed to comprehend her dreams and feelings. I've also done that in other aspects of my life. I was so consumed with my thoughts and inner turmoil that I couldn't hear answers to my prayers. I wondered how long must I wait.

Gail enrolled in a local college the next year and spent three years at home, working and going to school. During those years we experienced some of the most joyful times of our lives. Those memories still cause my heart to dance. The reality is that my plan would have deprived us of three wonderful years. God's plan was at work. He knew what the end would be, and I didn't. Every time I think about those three years, I am compelled to stop and thank the Almighty for allowing me to live His plan.

One big task was coping with well-meaning people trying to solve all my problems with a single Bible verse or cliché. I am sure you've already experienced this, if you're attending services on a regular basis. The one that wore me out was "Count it all joy." Frequently on Sunday, Wednesday night Bible study, or at the Fellowship of Christian Women's meeting, this "count it all joy" cliché would surface, and explanations were generously offered in all sincerity. I often thought about not attending the functions, but I was determined not to let the devil win—or, as my mother would say, "Don't let the devil put his paw on it." I continued to attend and wrestle with the concept and frequently ended up in tears of frustration. I'm sharing this with you because I know you are experiencing some of the same things, or you know someone who is. I couldn't figure out how I could find joy without Gail.

One Tuesday night, while attending a Fellowship of Christian Women's meeting, the discussion came up about how, whatever our trials are, we are to "count it all joy." I tried not to participate but found myself overreacting. These discussions are designed to help us understand and grow. Oversimplification always touches a nerve with me. We all need something we can embrace. Simple explanations are great until you're wrestling daily with your personal life-changing trial. All of us have heard the expression: *God may not come when you want Him, but He's always on time.* At the most intense moment of our discussion and explanations of "count it all joy," God sent our new pastor by. He was just sticking his head in to say hello to the group before leaving for the evening. Since I was talking when he came by, I told him that "count it all joy" was one of the thorns in my side. Am I to be happy that God took my daughter? Should I be clicking my heels like Dorothy in the Wizard of Oz, when she discovered how to get back to Kansas? How am I to get there from here? It's probably a good thing that I couldn't read his mind, because he was probably thinking, *It's not that complicated.* The pastor's perspective on this verse was simple, clear, and plain. He explained that the joy they're referring to simply means accepting that our trials are a part of God's plan.

What a relief and revelation for me. I had "counted it all joy" from the moment my beloved Gail flatlined and joined God in heaven. I just didn't know or understand the biblical context of joy. Through the numbness, shock, disbelief, and the shattering of my very being, I had talked to God and let Him know, "I don't like this or understand it, but I know it's in Your plan." I had no idea that counting it all joy was just acknowledging His plan. I believe God revealed that to me in His own time. I know His time and our time is different. God ordained that moment when He would reveal Himself at our meeting. I hope, as you deal with your loss, that this is one concept that you won't have to spend years trying to understand. Any relief you can get at this stage is welcomed.

....

"The years teach much which the days never knew."

RALPH WALDO EMERSON

....

Part III.

TRIBUTE IS YOUR THERAPY

This section is designed to honor, remember, and pay tribute to your beloved and to move you to a higher level of healing. I'm not suggesting that you will emerge from this exercise and be miraculously healed. I believe that as long as you exist, you will be in the healing process. I am suggesting that this can be a launching pad for the long journey of healing you must embark on to emerge from that grief-laden cocoon as a beautiful butterfly. The curtain has fallen on that beloved familiar role that was as comfortable as my favorite house slippers. This new production is starting without a dress rehearsal. I loved the role of being mom to such an energetic, loving, hardworking, and caring young lady. Suddenly it's a new day. I could not envision in my wildest dreams that this was my final curtain call in this role. The set, my lines, and my new character are all unfamiliar territory. Who am I supposed to be? I'm stepping out on faith. Faith also has a new face, like every other aspect of my life. Faith has changed from a feeling into an action. Suddenly my faith is all I have to lean on, and it dictates my every action or lack of action. *Oh Lord, please let my faith be strong.*

The tribute can take any form that works for you. You can honor or pay tribute to your beloved with a letter, poem, song, book, drawing, charitable contribution, plant, statute, or a hundred other forms that express your love. The beauty of this tribute is that it doesn't have to meet anyone's approval or needs but yours. It is "lovingly correct," and that's sufficient. My tribute to Gail is a happy place we shared. We both had a love for the written word in numerous forms. We always enjoyed good books, literature, letters, and e-mail. One of the great joys in my life was passing my appreciation for reading and books on to Gail. It was one of the most cherished gifts my mother gave me. My mother taught for fifty years at the middle school level and would have continued, had retirement not been required at age seventy. Even after spending all day in the classroom, she found time to teach each of her four children to read before we entered school.

Gail and I had a private book club. Our book club had a grand total of two members. We weren't looking for other members. We were both always reading a new book. When either of us found ourselves entrenched in an intriguing book, we would put pressure on the other to hurry up and finish her book, so we could pass it on. During the now-cherished week I spent with Gail before her beautiful daughter was born, I spent every spare moment completing her last book. She would ask if I was to this or that part yet. If I was, we would have a lively exchange; if not, I would say, "Don't tell me." I continue to be an avid reader, although it's not the same as sharing the adventure with Gail.

My tribute to Gail is a letter. Writing to or receiving a letter from her always gave a refreshing, sweet aura to my soul. Oh, to recapture that feeling, if only for a split second. My second tribute is a porcelain doll that I sculpted in her image.

As long as I can remember, I've always loved dolls. I had the best-cared-for dolls in town when I was a little girl. My love for dolls is still alive and well.

I had been working on sculpting several dolls for three years before my darling Gail departed. I believe my husband was convinced that I just liked playing with the clay and that completion of a doll was not my goal. My daughter always said, "Mom, you will finish your doll one day." It was a long pregnancy, but Gail, you were right. I did finish my doll, and she looks like you. The dress that she wears is a replica of your dad's favorite dress when you were a toddler, along with the two braids and fat cheeks. My favorite doll will forever be my doll named Gail. Sculpting her has been a "source of joy."

Chapter 10

A LETTER TO MY DAUGHTER, GAIL (A SOURCE OF JOY)

"I thank my God upon every remembrance of you."

PHILIPPIANS 1:3

My Dearest Gail:

From the first glance at your beautiful face twenty-seven years ago, I somehow knew that there was something magnificent about you. At the time I passed it off as the maternal feeling that is spoken and written about all the time. I knew that we had chosen the perfect name for this gift from heaven, because Gail means "a source of joy," and I was bubbling over with joy. Heaven was sending me a signal that this was no ordinary child that I had been given.. The absence of a single labor pain during your birth was a miracle in itself. That didn't distract me from my amazement over my perfect little baby girl. Regardless of your age, I guess that's why, among the many little names of endearment I had for you, "baby girl" was my favorite..

There was no greater joy for me than to be in your presence. Your presence, not the event or activity, is what always made the moment special." We always kept a special place that was shared by just the two of us. This place could be entered with a glance across a crowded room, a shared expression that was reserved for the two of us, a shopping trip, lunch, or both of us dialing the phone at the same time and getting a busy signal. We shared something that I can't put into words, but it enriched my life beyond any expectation that this earthly life offers. I am eternally grateful for the gift that God gave me when He created you and trusted me to be your mom.

Caring for you, whether it was noon or midnight, was a cherished moment. I always felt so thankful and honored for the privilege.

These are the thoughts you never share for fear of sounding ridiculous. Occasionally I ventured out and shared with you that private place, closely guarded and tucked away, that captures the essence of my spirit. You appreciated the honesty and the glimpse into my soul. That was that heavenly quality and maturity that you always displayed and I always loved. That type of wisdom is rare in the young. Your dad frequently spoke of that "special thing" that we shared. Oh, how I miss it! I realize that's one blessing I can only cherish, because I'll never be able to share it again. It was uniquely ours.

When you were three years old, I sent you off to preschool three mornings a week. I sent you because it was best for you, but I missed you terribly. I realized that my "baby girl" was taking her first steps toward independence. I could hardly wait to drive around the circle and pick you up from the steps that sprawled around the front of the building. During dismissal time it was always lined with thirty little angels. Your big, beautiful brown eyes always got even bigger than usual when you first spotted your mommy's car. I used to love that moment, because I was just as excited as you were. I remember the day I pulled around the circle, and you were crying your little eyes out. Without a second thought, I stopped my car and jumped out, forcing every other proud parent lined up on the circle to come to a dead stop and wait even longer to pickup their little ones. As I raced up to the steps, my heart was pounding. *Dear God, let Gail be okay.* When I reached the steps, you were sobbing so hard you could not speak, but you were pointing and frightened beyond belief. At about the same time as I reached you, one of the teachers came running over, and we both spotted the *ladybug* on your dress at the same time. I fell in love with ladybugs at that moment. I prayed that all your problems in life would be as easy as removing a ladybug from your dress. My stock really increased in value for you, as we shared one of our special mom-daughter moments. One thing is certain: we never lacked wonderful moments.

As the years progressed, I was fascinated by how differently we cherished the same moment. Your heart was storing and cradling life through a little girl's eyes, and I was experiencing life through the eyes of an adult. Certain treasured moments are permanently tucked safely in the chamber of my heart that will always have *Gail* etched on it in bold letters.

Most moments on the steps outside your preschool at the end of a busy morning were happy ones. One day in particular turned out to be second only to Christmas morning. As our car entered the circle lineup for pickup, you were about to have a big, happy surprise. Your dad was off work this particular day, and he was picking you up. The opposite of the ladybug trauma was experienced that morning—and talked about for the next twenty-four years. The angels must have created the father-daughter relationship you shared. It was angelic.

Gail, we had so many joyous moments, and still I ache for just one more. I've revisited many of our treasured moments and have to say, girl, we gave it our all. I smile when I envision your little fat cheeks and eyes of wonder. How could someone be so special and innocent? Kindergarten held as much wonderment for me as it did for you.

Do you remember our first parent-teacher conference, and your teacher wondering why you were allowed to stay up so late that you often fell asleep on your mat during your brief quiet time? I hated to break up the freshly polished September professionalism of your little young, fresh-out-of college, enthusiastic teacher. Her name escapes me after all these years. Before she laid her profound wisdom on me, concerning the proper bedtime for a five year old, I let her know your bedtime was 7:30 p.m., and you usually took a long nap after lunch. That's why you were moved from the afternoon class to the morning class and allowed to still enjoy your afternoon nap. I used to say that's why you were so pretty, because you took your "beauty rest" seriously.

In 1976 the bicentennial celebration in your first-grade class was one of those special moments that we embraced differently. With the wide-eyed innocence and sincerity of a saint, you wanted an answer to a question that you had been wondering about all afternoon. As you ran through the door after school and saw me, your burning question jumped out of your mouth. "Mom, were you around during colonial times?" Without blinking, I said "No." You were just six years old, but that day I learned that our ages were light years apart. That was a moment when I recaptured the child in myself. What a joy. Seeing the world through the eyes of a child is a blessing unto itself.

That was also the same year that "Rouge Rabbit" was officially born and recognized as one of the endearing names we gave you. I know you'll chuckle when you remember staying with Grandma Parks when your dad and I went on vacation. Even at six years old, you had learned that my mom was from the "old school." When it came to makeup and perfume, you thought it was important enough to take a chance. What is life without some risk? As Mother was walking out the door leaving for church and glanced back, she spotted "Baby Girl" in full makeup. I was told that it took only one "old school" glance, and you were up the steps, washed your face, and were back out the door headed to church with gold medal speed. What's the problem with a six-year-old wearing makeup? We finally had to deal with the reality that "Rouge Rabbit" never saw a cosmetic, perfume, or jewelry department that she could pass up. I would have never experienced the pampering and special joy of a makeover had God not blessed me with you.

Little did I know that you were going to follow up with the project of all projects that same year. From the day we learned that you existed, months before you were born, your dad and I imagined what this little perfect being would aspire to be. You brought us crashing down with a reality check with that top-secret first-grade project. After six weeks of anticipating the revelation and surprise of "What I Want to Be When I Grow Up," the day arrived. You were allowed to bring home your project at the end of the quarter. You were never good at keeping secrets, but you fooled even yourself this time. I'll never forget seeing you, running down the hill from the school playground and racing in with the pride of a newly crowned champion. You handed me the masterpiece, and in bold letters it stated, "When I grow up, I want to be the Avon Lady."

I'll never know how I managed to reach down and pick my heart up off the floor, muster up a smile, and praise you on your project at the same time. As the years rolled by, that project gave us more shared laughs than we would ever be able to count. My first chuckle came when you made me promise not to tell Dad when he came home from work, because it was your surprise. I thought, *Be my guest.* Your dad handled the surprise with dignity and class on the outside, but I knew exactly what his true feelings were. *How do we motivate this child to consider other options?*

When we mixed it up together around our kitchen table or in a quiet girlie moment, I experienced a glimpse of heaven; and my faith tells me that you're in a place where you can laugh all day around the kitchen table. Your presence in our home just seemed to radiate throughout the room, and there was joy in the air. I'm trying with every ounce of strength I can muster up to not be sad and rejoice in your heavenly victory. More often than not, I fail. Knowing me like you do, you understand. I know I'm rambling in this letter. We always did that in letters and e-mails to each other. I'm not about to tamper with something that has always worked for us. Our letters were never concerned with English 101, but they were centered with a big scoop of "She'll know what I'm saying." That was our style. My mind is all over the place as I remember your earthly journey.

What about the mother-daughter basketball game we played in when you were ten? I don't know who was prouder, you or me. We were equally surprised at how well I could play, even though I played it off. I hadn't played in many years, but I'd never before or since had the privilege of playing with you. Please keep your skills polished up, because I'm going to challenge you to a game of twenty-one when we get together. You know how both of us loved "memory lane." I'm not about to give that up—and you better not, either.

I've decided a trip down memory lane wouldn't be complete without touching on those wonderful teen years of yours. I still believe some of those times when you broke curfew, you were just waiting in the driveway until you were late. I'll give you credit, you always stated your position with gusto, got grounded for another week, and stormed down the hall to your room. Of course, you always made it clear before leaving that you were the only one among your friends who had a curfew. I always replied, "You're the only one that lives in my house and puts your feet under my table." At those times I could see myself in you, and I chuckled inside. The big difference was that in my day, I could only think the things you verbalized. Freedom of speech wasn't practiced with parents in my generation.

The beauty of those incidents is a quality we share. Neither of us could ever stay upset or angry for long. I can still see you coming back down the hallway after about five or ten minutes and saying, "Well, since I'm grounded for a week, what are we going to do?" I would pretend and say, "Nothing, because I'm upset with you." You would hug me with those long, skinny arms and say, "Oh, you know you love me, and you're not angry." We'd laugh and embrace, and that would be the end of it. We weren't capable of sustained anger with each other, but we sure could work it for five or ten minutes. I cherished that quality in you and realized it was unique long before you went to heaven. Your father and I frequently talked about how blessed we were that God had given us such a wonderful daughter—but more importantly, a wonderful friend.

The beautiful, mature adult you became will always be one of my great sources of joy. I marveled at how you could focus on a problem or situation and move forward. You always seemed to be able to see the forest, while others were focusing on the trees. Nothing seemed impossible for you once you made up your mind. I watched you work fifty to sixty hours a week, go to school at night, sacrifice clothes and jewelry, and never complain, as you helped your husband through school.

You were our "Baby Girl," but when any other member of the family was struggling with life, you were the one who brought him or her back to the center. You were always able to embrace the issue.

Lord knows you loved a good debate. You knew how to disagree
without being disagreeable. I'll always treasure the debate you and
your father had Thanksgiving Day 1997—our thirty-second wedding anniversary and also our last holiday with you—even though
I told both of you to just shut up. As usual, the two of you ignored
my comment. It was like I was talking to the wall. Neither of you
was about to walk away from a debate where the generation gap
between the two of you would never allow you to agree. This type
of debate always seemed to energize both of you. It was like you two
were "letting the good times roll." A stranger would have thought
you two were arguing, but these debates were never infused with
anger. You and your dad loved and respected each other too much
for that. This was one of the few areas you and I rarely shared.

Gail, words are so inadequate to express my grief over your
earthly departure to heaven. I want to lie across the bed and discuss
our plans and dreams for the future, exchange and discuss the lat-
est book we've read, e-mail you and receive e-mail from you, go to
church together, marvel at your beautiful daughter Brianna, shop
with you, attend your graduation, hug and kiss you, cook a meal
with you, meet your friends, take a trip together, sit on Mother's
front porch and have a "hen party," rejoice in your accomplish-
ments, be a good listener when you need an ear, share birthday and
holiday celebrations, and a million other things. Most of all, I just
want to love you unconditionally.

I know you'll understand that's the human side of me. You
know me well enough to know that I don't understand the big picture or even claim to. I'm thankful that God allowed you to spend
twenty-seven glorious years with us.

I have spent countless hours and shed buckets of tears trying
to understand why God would take you back. I still don't know,
but after fourteen years, I realize your mission was complete. God
opened my heart and my eyes and said, "Look around you." As I
looked around, I realized that everything you touched, you left
better than the way you found it. The fruits of your labor are still

being felt and enjoyed by people you never met. You have touched and lifted the quality of life for many. The benefits of your efforts are like the rising tide that lifts all boats. You surely lifted the quality of my life and allowed me to experience love on a level that words would diminish. Your loss forced me to be stronger than I imagined I was capable of being. Survival for me has been defined.

One of the comfort places in my life is the fact that you were a Christian, and I know you're in heaven. I know that your short stay with us is a part of God's plan, and I won't understand it until I, too, am in heaven by His side. I don't know how to thank you for such sweet memories, so I'll just say...thank you. Thanks for being the sweet, loving daughter who was so thoughtful and generous in all endeavors. I truly believe you were an angel. The signs were all around, but I think God knew I was not capable of recognizing or handling it. It would have been much too overwhelming for me. We always shared an openness and frankness, so please note: I said angel, not saint.

Every time I am physically or mentally in the presence of your beautiful daughter Brianna, I know that your legacy is in good hands. One look into her big brown eyes, and I am sure that she too is "a source of joy." She is loving, sensitive, intelligent, and beautiful like her mother. Thanks for leaving us with such a precious gift. It is just like you to go overboard with a gift. I adore her, and she knows that she is Maw Maw's doll baby. I will always honor you by making sure that your daughter knows the unique person her mother was. With all the heartbreak and tears that the storm has dumped in our laps, this opportunity to share with your most precious gift presents a magnificent, beautiful rainbow in our lives.

I guess I have rambled on long enough for now, so I will close the way I did December 9, 1997, in our last conversation. I love you, sweet pea. Your response, *I love you more,* will forever embrace my heart.

I hope you like the doll. Thanks for always having confidence that I would one day complete my dolls.

Gail, you are always loved.

....

"Thy faith hath saved thee; go in peace."

L U K E 7 : 5 0

....

Ten Things I Learned During My Journey

- Find joy in taking small steps forward.
- The timeline for regaining a sense of normalcy will be different for each person.
- Expect long periods of mental exhaustion. They will come and they will go.
- Turn to your inner strength and core beliefs to avoid feeling overwhelmed. Healthy distractions should be your goal.
- Find healthy distractions by embracing friends, hobbies, and loved ones.
- Knowing exactly how long it will take to regain your balance should not be your focus. The real priority is in defining, for yourself, the terms of your recovery. What is it, and how will you know when you have arrived?
- The life you once knew has changed forever, but at an emotional and spiritual level, you must do all that you can to reserve a place for hope and optimism.
- Strengthen your faith and accept that this is not your plan, but the plan of a much higher power.
- Remember, you are in a marathon, not a sprint. There will be brief moments of peace and calm. Use this time wisely.
- Find specific ways, throughout the year, to honor your lost loved one. It is a crucial step in filling the gaping hole left behind by the death of a loved one, and it is therapeutic.

My husband wrote the following short essay in 1998, following Gail's passing. He wrote it as a tribute to Gail. It was also an admission that growing up as one of five boys can leave plenty of room for learning, when it comes to rearing a daughter.

Lessons I Learned from My Daughter
By Lin Hart

It was time for a change and I was ready to make a big one. I did what many baby boomers were dreaming of doing. I left the security of the corporate nest and joined the ranks of those brave souls starting a second career. I thought, "Why not?" Times were good, and I had a burning desire to speak to the issues of the day. Corporations were beckoning for experienced voices to help them shape their message as they dashed headlong into the twenty-first century.

Today, I am a full-time professional speaker. Since joining the ranks of the thousands of speakers who make up the industry, I have been amazed to find that most people are surprised to hear that one could actually become a professional speaker. The standard response is, "Oh, you mean you are a public speaker." My counter is, "No. Public speakers speak free. I speak for a living. You see, if I don't speak, I don't eat." That's the first hard lesson one learns when one runs off to join the ranks of the self-employed. Of course, there are many positives, but that is a subject for another article.

Professional speakers provide a valuable service. They speak to people about stuff people should actually be reading about. Contrary to popular belief, reading is good for you. It is a great way to find wisdom and feed the mind. Most people feel reading takes too long; it is a lot easier to sit and listen to someone speak. The professional speaker's challenge is to find and deliver the wisdom and deeper meaning people are seeking. Oddly enough, the source of much of the speaker's wisdom comes from simple day-to-day experiences. These are the gems that ordinary people either miss or simply choose to ignore. It is the speaker's job to find, assemble, and deliver these gems to the audience.

In many ways, listening to a professional speaker is like listening to an audio book. The difference is that the professional speaker shows up in person, costs a lot more, and you cannot shut them off if you do not like them. Of course, you can always walk out, but most people are too polite to go to that extreme.

Living and Learning. At the outset of my speaking career, I learned that being able to find and distill wisdom from one's own life is the key to becoming a great speaker. One of the country's top humorists and a friend, Grady Jim Robinson, told me that the gift of all great speakers is that they are able to glean learning and wisdom from their own journey through life. This learning forms the bricks and mortar of all great speeches. It is at this point when professional speaking can serve as a mirror of life. By sharing his or her personal stories, a speaker can make a difference in someone else's life. A speaker's true brilliance comes through when he or she is able to translate his or her life's learning into a meaningful message that every listener in the audience can relate to. This special talent is one of the main reasons Bill Cosby and Art Linkletter have long been admired as great speakers.

While you may not be a professional speaker, it seems to me there is enormous value in thinking of your life's journey as a journey of learning. I have always thought of living and learning as being inseparable. You cannot have one without the other. Think for a moment. If you were suddenly called upon to give the biggest speech of your life, from where would you draw your learning? What have been the sources of your life's learning? What relationships have had the greatest influence in your life?

My Learning Story. For me, there have been many learning experiences, but one stands out more today than any other in my life. It began on July 14, 1970, and was actually the beginning of a series of experiences. This was the day our daughter Gail was born. She was our second child, and she held the distinction of being the first little girl to enter my previously male-dominated life. Having grown up in a family of five brothers and no sisters, Gail was really a big deal for me. She was so special, I felt I had to come up with my own special nickname for my incredibly awesome daughter. I do not really remember when it started, but I began calling her "Worlds." It just sounded right, and I felt good saying it. The nickname "Worlds" stuck. Calling Gail "Worlds" was my way of saying, "You are the world's most beautiful daughter." It became our secret term of endearment.

To understand what all this was about, you had to know Gail. From the time she was born, she was special. Aside from being cute as the dickens, she was a smart, fun-loving, and precocious child. Growing up, she always had a big light bulb smile that lit up wherever she went. As a teenager she was curious, smart, and funny, and she liked being with her daddy.

Given my past and the lack of female siblings in my life, getting the hang of things with Gail was, initially, a little intimidating. Like many men of my generation (baby boomers), I had always thought of little girls as nice to have around, but they were, for the most part, mom's little buddy. What can they do? They cannot play sports. They will not like hanging out with their dad and their brothers. It was as if I was locked in the stone age.

Learning Hits High Gear. It was at this point that my learning began. As soon as her little feet hit the ground, Gail began the systematic destruction of all of Dad's stereotypical notions about girls and young women. As a toddler, she kept up with both Dad and her big brother. As a youngster, she shagged fly balls, kept up, and was never afraid to try something new. As she grew older, my son and I agreed that Gail would never be left out of anything just because she was a girl. As a teenager, she was a great softball and basketball player, a bundle of laughs, and, on top of all of that, she grew into a beautiful young woman. She became her mom's best friend and a close confidant to her dad and her brother.

As Gail reached adulthood, the pace of my learning quickened. During our often spirited conversations, she would vigorously debate my point of view on music, current dress, popular events, and political correctness. Gail's probing and sometimes even provocative way of asking questions would often lead me to a more sensitive and tolerant view of the younger generation. In retrospect, I now see that she softened my hard positions to something more appropriate for the times we were living in. The world always seemed a little less complex and more hopeful when viewed through the filter she provided. While we did not always agree, I was often challenged to see the world from a different perspective. I was learning, and I did not realize it at the time.

Getting beyond Fatherhood. At some point during my journey with Gail, it occurred to me that my learning was extending beyond just learning how to become a good father. Unknowingly, I had begun learning how to become a better person. Gail's journey had become intertwined with that of my own.

Over the years, I have been in a constant search for wisdom, understanding, and learning. Gail provided me with so much to draw from. Being her father and friend has truly been a blessing. Her lessons were many, but these are the ones that meant the most to me:

- Being a good father requires learning to expect the unexpected.
- Do not confuse your title with the real purpose of your work. Being a great father is about more than just being a breadwinner.
- Success is gender neutral.
- Judging people is bad, but prejudging (prejudice) is worse.
- An open show of affection and love is an act of strength, not weakness.
- Given the choice, a woman's intuition is usually better than a man's pride (especially when seeking directions).
- Actions alone are not enough. If you do not tell people how you feel, they will never really know.

- The gift of life is not for living in the past or in the future. The gift of life is for living in the *now*!
- Knee-high tube socks do not make the same fashion statement today as they did in the '80s. There comes a time when you have to change.

As my relationship with my daughter grew, I began changing many of my previously held stereotypical views about females. Today, much of what I have learned stems directly from my journey with Gail. These lessons have now become a part of the fabric that makes up my value system. They have served as the lens through which I have viewed women in my personal and professional life.

The Tough Lessons. As I write these words, I am dealing with living the most difficult experience any parent could have. It is an experience that no parent wants to be confronted with. On December 13, 1997, Gail passed away. As her father, friend, and admirer, her death has been an incredibly difficult blow. There is no way to describe the hurt and the loss. Family, friends, and those who knew Gail have all suffered along with us as we have tried to cope with the empty chasm that such a loss leaves.

As jolting as this loss has been, I do take some comfort in knowing that Gail taught me so much while she was here. In her passing, I have also learned another valuable lesson. You and I possess tremendous personal power. It is personal power that, if used positively, can allow each of us to make an enormous difference in someone else's life. What we learn from our life's journey can sometimes come at a high price. How we deal with it can become the source of our greatest gift to someone else. This is something the truly great speakers have always understood.

Therefore, I ask you: If you were called upon today, to give the speech of your life, what part of your life's journey could you draw upon for inspiration and motivation? What are the sources of your learning? Would it make a suitable gift for someone else?

A New Teacher Arrives. I think Gail always considered me a work in progress. There was so much more she wanted to teach me, but there just was not enough time. Still, as one might expect, Gail made certain this base was covered before leaving. She is, no doubt, observing this very moment, while my new teacher begins setting up the classroom, dusting off the textbooks, and laying out the lesson plan. You see, three weeks before leaving on her journey to heaven, Gail blessed us with a beautiful little granddaughter. Now, little Brianna Nicole has the job of teaching her dad and her granddad. She is serious about her work, too. Just as dutifully as was her mom, Brianna wakes me up every morning with a cry that says, "Front and center, Granddad, class is now in session."

For the fathers reading this article, I have a special caution for you. Stay alert! You can learn the darnedest things from your daughters (and your granddaughters).

Thank you, Gail.

Thank you for the learning!

Lin Hart, Copyright ©1998, Lin Hart & Associates, October 1, 1998